OUTSTANDING
ART IDEAS
for Kids Grades 4-6

Gail Tuchman

Troll Associates

Interior Illustrations by: Marilyn Barr

ISBN: 0-8167-2596-9

Printed in the United States of America.

10   9   8   7   6   5   4   3   2

CONTENTS

May

June/July/August

INTRODUCTION

With this book, children will turn tin cans into wind chimes, soda bottles into terrariums, cornhusks into coasters, and twigs into looms for weaving. Common, inexpensive and natural materials—from paper clips to acorns—will be transformed into art.

Outstanding Art Ideas for Kids: Grades 4–6 offers you a wide range of hands-on art activities to share with your class, all of which will help to develop children's awareness of their own creative capabilities. The ideas will challenge children and encourage them to strengthen their skills.

These activities are arranged from September through the summer. Some projects offer ideas for holidays and seasonal activities. Others can be used at any time, in conjunction with lessons being taught. (For example, making a class patchwork quilt can tie in with studies about the pioneers.) For each month, Activity Sheets are included. These are addressed to children and include all the information they need to do fun independent projects. Teachers can simply photocopy Activity Sheets and distribute them to children.

Each project lists the materials you'll need and provides simple instructions. The step-by-step instructions are directly transferrable to the child for a ready-made art lesson. Before you begin a project, read through the directions, gather all materials, and set aside a block of time. You might call in parents or other volunteers to help children with projects, as needed.

Children will learn a variety of different art techniques: paper crafting, papier-mâché, painting, printing, patchwork, puppetry, collage, nature craft, rubbings, weaving, embossing, tie-dye, sculpture, sewing, mosaics and mobiles. They'll also explore many media: clay, cans, paper, paints, burlap, wire, soap, and materials from nature. Although the projects yield specific products, the process will open the way to using the techniques and materials for other kinds of artwork in the future.

The ideas will tap the children's imaginations and interests and provide them with basic techniques they can use whenever they have the impulse to create art. After learning a technique, children should be encouraged to experiment with it, and to create all sorts of variations. As children learn to manipulate new materials, their own natural ingenuity will be awakened, resulting in ideas for original designs and objects.

The projects emphasize recycling and reusing materials, such as bottles, bags, metal cans, cardboard tubes, newspaper, scraps of string, fabric, and yarn. Consider setting up a classroom recycling area. Encourage children to bring in materials that can be recycled into art projects and sort them into cartons. Whenever a project calls for these objects, they'll be right at hand. Ask your principal to request recycled paper when ordering school supplies.

Check all arts and crafts materials to make sure they do not present any health hazards for children by ingestion, inhalation, or skin contact. Always use water-based markers, glues, and paints, and talc-free, premixed clays. Never use solvent-based adhesives like rubber cement, or solvents like shellac. Use watercolor, liquid tempera, or acrylic paints. Make sure that paints do not contain toxic pigments, such as cadmiums and vermillions.

Inhaling dusts and powders from dry clay and plaster can be hazardous to children. Yet such projects as casting may be done by children if the steps that are potentially hazardous are removed. For example, you can mix powdered tempera with water in a well-ventilated area when children are not present. Plaster casting should never be done of body parts, because the plaster can cause severe burns.

The Labeling of Hazardous Art Materials Act, a United States law, requires that warning labels appear on art materials with chronic hazards as well as acute hazards. Such materials are inappropriate for children to use. There is available a list of publications about art hazards and safety precautions for elementary school children. To obtain this list, send a self-addressed stamped envelope to:

Center for Safety in the Arts
5 Beekman Street
New York, NY 10038

The projects in **Oustanding Art Ideas for Kids: Grades 4-6** are enjoyable for teachers and children alike. Each project leads to improvisation with various materials and art techniques; and this improvisation is sure to result in many new, exciting projects.

Grateful acknowledgment is made to Barbara Packer for permission to use many of the ideas we created together.

G.T.

What You Need

measuring cup

mixing bowl

spoon

flour, salt, cold water

food coloring

pencils

empty tin can (to hold pencils while working and drying)

white glue

tempera and paintbrushes

flat thin piece of wood or sheet of cardboard for base, about 6 inches x 9 inches (about 15 cm x 23 cm)

Flour 'n' Salt School Supplies

Pencil Toppings and Pen and Pencil Holders

What You Do

Making the Dough

1. Tell students they can cook up back-to-school supplies from flour and salt. When the dough-clay dries, the objects will become hard. Make the self-hardening clay by mixing together 1 cup (250 ml) flour and 1 cup (250 ml) salt. (See note on coloring clay, Step 3, before continuing.) Gradually stir in *cold* water to create a mixture with a good consistency for modeling. Knead the clay by hand.

2. When the mixture is no longer sticky, it's ready. If the dough is too dry, add more water. If it's sticky, add more flour and salt. The recipe yields the approximate amount of clay needed for one pencil topping and holder. If necessary, make more clay by mixing equal parts of flour and salt with cold water.

3. The objects can be painted after they're dry. Or color can be added before objects are shaped:
   a. Add food coloring to the water before mixing the water with flour and salt.
   b. Or divide the dough into four or five balls, one for each color. Flatten each ball and add a few drops of food coloring. Knead the color into the clay.

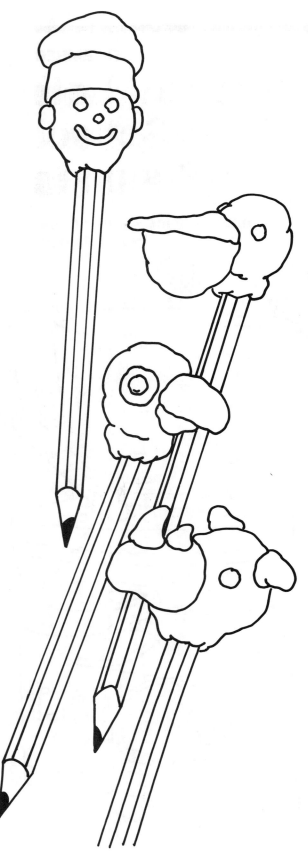

Pencil Toppings

1. Shape the clay into a 3/4-inch (2-cm) ball. Insert the eraser end of a pencil into the middle of the ball, twisting it to make the hole slightly larger. Make sure the pencil doesn't poke through the other end of the clay.

2. Encourage children to use their imaginations to create their pencil toppings. Shapes can be fashioned right on the pencil. (To work a shape, put the pencil down when working on the front of it, hold the clay ball in the palm of one hand, or rest the pencil upright in a tin can.)

3. Try rolling out small pieces of clay hair. Shape small clay pieces into facial features. Add special features such as a pelican's pouch, a toucan's beak, or a rhino's horn. Put a chef's hat onto a head. Pieces can be glued or pressed onto the ''head.''

4. Set the pencil in a tin can and allow the shape to dry on the pencil. When the clay is dry, use tempera to add additional color or details. Children can make as many pencil toppings as they like.

Pen and Pencil Holders

1. Use a piece of wood or cardboard as a base. Shape a large ball of clay—about 4 inches (10 cm) in diameter—into an animal. The central part of the body must be sturdy and deep enough—at least 1 1/2 inches (4 cm) thick—to hold the pen and pencils.

2. Children can use pictures of animals as references for shaping bodies. Some suggestions are porcupines, hippos, ducks, swans, and kittens. As a challenge, try a kangaroo with a pouch! Use the pointed end of a pencil as a modeling tool to make deep-set eyes, feathers, wings, or fish scales. Press or glue on clay parts, working with different colors.

3. When the animal is shaped, insert the eraser end of a pencil into the holder and poke 5 or 6 holes for pencils and pens. Be careful not to poke through the bottom of the clay. Press the bottom edges of the animal onto the base, so it sticks. Allow the clay holder to dry thoroughly (for about a week).

4. Use tempera to paint the holder if color clay was not used or if additional color is desired. Let paint dry.

5. Insert pens and pencils into the holder. Top off the holder by adding a pencil with a flour 'n' salt topping. These pencil holders are *top*notch!

What You Need

dried cornhusks

dish or tray (for soaking dried cornhusks)

hot water

thin wire (flexible enough to bend into circle, strong enough to act as center frame for husks)

wire cutters

string, scissors, pencil, ruler

towel

wax paper

heavy book

nylon thread (for hanging)

Autumn Cornhusk Sunbursts

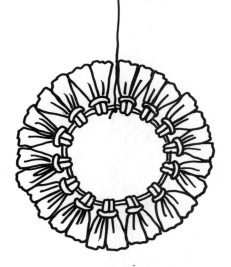

What You Use

1. Tell children that artists have captured sunbursts by making ornamental pins and other objects that have a central disk with rays emanating from it.

2. Since dried cornhusks tear easily and are not pliable, work with dampened husks. Soak the dried cornhusks in hot water for 10 to 15 minutes.

3. Make a center frame for the sunburst by bending a piece of wire into a circle about 4 inches (10 cm) in diameter. Tightly secure the wire ends together with string.

4. Remove cornhusks from the water and cut them along the ribs into pieces about 5 inches x 1/2 inch (12 1/2 cm x 1 cm). Cover the wet pieces with a damp towel to keep them moist.

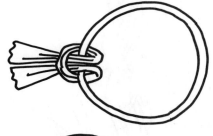

5. To tie a husk onto the wire frame, first fold it in half from top to bottom. Place the folded part of the husk under the frame and bring the ends up through the loop created by the fold. Pull tightly so that the husk is securely fastened to the wire.

6. Continue tying cornhusks to the frame so that each strand radiates from the center. As each new husk is added, push it up against the husk before it.

7. When the wire frame is completely tied with husks, place the sunburst between two pieces of wax paper and press flat between the pages of a very heavy book to dry. Hang the Autumn Cornhusks Sunburst from heavy nylon thread.

Corny Coasters

What You Need

cornhusks, dried (12 for each coaster)
dish or tray (for soaking dried cornhusks)
hot water
thin string
tapestry needle
twine (in autumn colors, if available)
scissors

What You Do

1. Cornhusks were used by Native Americans to make moccasins, baskets, mats, and other functional items. Tell students that they can save, dry, and then turn cornhusks into many useful things, such as coasters.

2. Soak the dried cornhusks in hot water for 10 to 15 minutes to soften them, then shake off the excess water. Use thin string to tie three husks together at one end. Braid the husks.

3. New husks will frequently need to be added to those being braided. To join a husk to one that's being braided, overlap the ends of the two husks, wrapping one piece well around the other so that the husks form one continuous strip.

4. Continue braiding until all twelve husks have been used.

5. Now Roll-a-Coaster! Roll the husks into an oval shape and sew the shape together with twine. Here's how: Thread the tapestry needle with twine and knot one end. Turn one end of the braided husks inward, wrapping it flatly around itself. Push the needle through the husks in the center until the knot rests against a coil.

overlap the ends of 2 husks

6. Wind the braided husks around a little more and sew over the coiled part toward the center.

7. Continue to make the circle bigger by wrapping and sewing as follows, making a figure eight stitch: Sew *over* one row (A), *under* the next row (B), *over* the same row (B), and *under* (A). Be sure to keep the coaster even and flat.

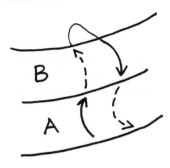

8. At the end, sew over the last piece and make a knot.

9. Tell students not to worry about the twine showing. It's supposed to. As they wrap and sew the braided husk together, they are creating a design with the twine. The twine becomes part of the coaster's appeal.

10. Students can make a set of coasters in this way. Or they can create a circular mat by enlarging a coaster.

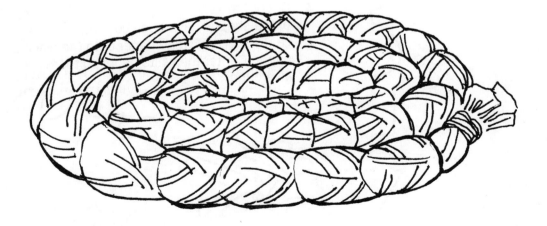

Paper Images

What You Do

Experimenting with paper, scissors, and glue can lead to many interesting designs. Try two ideas that follow the rule: *Add nothing—Take nothing away.* Tell students they'll keep all of the paper they begin with, but will change its form.

Mirror Images

1. Draw different shapes around the edges of a piece of white paper.

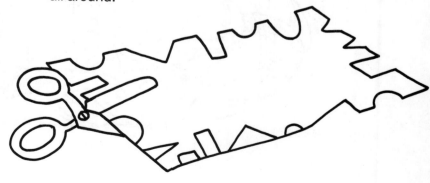

2. Cut out the shapes and place them in a pile. After all of the shapes have been cut out, glue the remaining center piece of white paper onto the piece of larger black paper. Center the white paper so there is equal space all around.

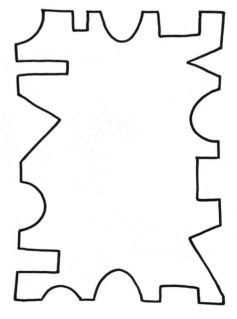

3. Insert the shapes you cut out back into their original places, but lift each shape and flip it back so that it is a mirror image of the cutout space. Glue each shape to the black background, making sure that the edge of the cutout space and the cutout piece line up.

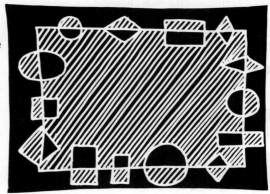

More Mirror Images

1. Try another mirror image idea. On the small piece of black paper draw a shape, such as an animal. Cut out the shape and any details. Glue the black paper, minus the cutouts, onto half of the white sheet of paper.

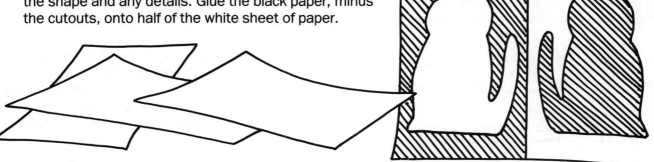

2. Place the black cutouts on the white paper opposite the missing shapes on the black side of the page. When the mirror image appears, glue the black cutouts onto the white half of the paper.

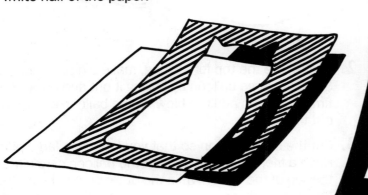

3. These ideas are only a beginning. Encourage students to improvise with paper images of their own. They can use the same rule or create another one.

Three-in-One Percussion Instrument

Instruments are played in different ways to make different sounds. Percussion instruments are played by shaking, striking, or scraping. Rattles, tambourines, drums, and triangles are all percussion instruments. You can make one percussion instrument that can be played in three different ways.

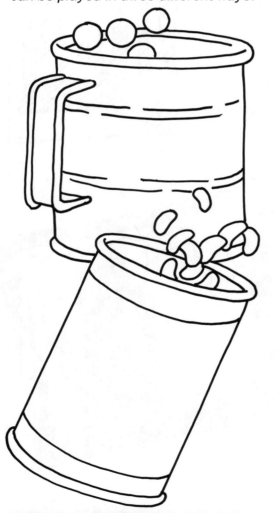

What You Need

metal flour sifter (a metal coffee can may be substituted)

handful of marbles, pebbles, beans, or beads

large round balloon (Ask an adult to blow up the balloon.)

scissors

string

colorful tape (or plain masking tape and markers or crayons)

2 wooden sticks (same length)

2 pieces of felt, sponge, or absorbent cotton

colorful yarn (several long pieces)

What You Do

1. To prepare the inside of the flour sifter for shaking, put into it a handful of marbles, pebbles, beans, or beads. These objects will knock against one another and vibrate freely to make different sounds when they are shaken or when the handle of the sifter is squeezed or cranked.

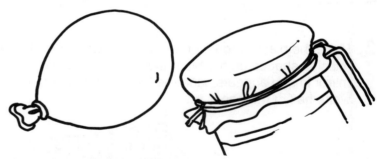

2. To prepare the top for striking, make a drumhead. Stretch a large balloon by pulling it out and back several times. (Ask an adult to blow up the balloon and then let out the air.)

3. Cut the balloon open so that you have one large piece. Have a friend help you stretch the balloon carefully over the top of the sifter. While the other person holds the stretched balloon in place, secure it tightly by winding string below the rim of the sifter. Wrap the string around several times and then knot the ends together.

4. Use strips of colorful tape to decorate the sides of the instrument. (Or use plain masking tape and color it with crayons or markers.) Leave plenty of metal space so you can rub against the sides with wooden sticks to create musical sounds.

5. You can use wooden sticks as drumsticks. You might want to pad one end of the stick before you strike it against the drumhead. Try tying either a small wad of felt, a sponge piece, or absorbent cotton to one end of the stick. The stick will create a different sound when the end is padded. You can also try beating the drum with the eraser end of a pencil, or even the dried bone of a turkey drumstick.

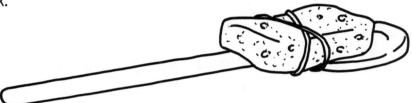

6. Add a strap. Tie several pieces of yarn onto the handle of the sifter to form a big loop that goes over your head and extends to your waist. It's a handy way to carry the instrument.

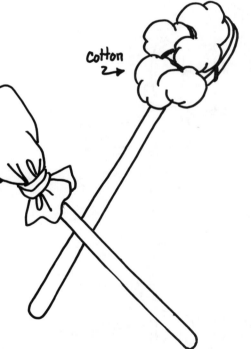

Cotton →

Playing the Instrument—Three Ways

Experimentation is the key to making different sounds with your instrument.

1. Strike (tap) the instrument on the drumhead.

2. Shake the instrument, or squeeze or crank the handle.

3. Scrape (rub) the metal sides of the instrument with a ruler, pencil, or chopstick.

Play your Three-in-One Percussion Instrument to the rhythmic beat of some music. Maybe you and some friends would enjoy forming a homemade instrument band!

Ojo de Dios and Twisted Twig Weavings

What You Need

2 sticks or drinking straws, 8 inches (20 cm) long for each Ojo de Dios Weaving

yarn (different colors); avoid very thick yarn

scissors

masking tape

white glue

ruler

twigs with many twisting branching shoots—for Twig Weavings (use twigs that have fallen from trees)

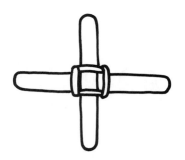

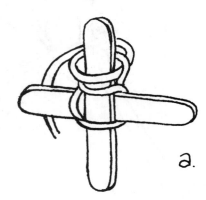

a.

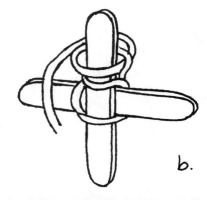

b.

What You Do

Ojo de Dios (God's Eye)

1. Tell students that this colorful stick-and-yarn weaving—Ojo de Dios or God's Eye—is made by the Huichol Indians in Mexico. The ornament has been described as a symbol for "seeing" and "understanding" and carries with it a wish for long life. These weavings are made for a special festival in October.

2. Cross two 8-inch (20-cm) sticks or straws at the center. Secure them in place by tying together the sticks or straws securely with a piece of yarn.

3. To weave, begin at the center. Wrap the yarn in one of these ways. Each way makes a different design:
   a. Wind around, looping the yarn *over* one stick (straw) and completely around it, then *under* another stick and completely around it. Continue weaving in a counterclockwise circle in this manner.
   b. Wind the yarn *over* and completely around one stick (straw), and *over* and completely around the next stick.

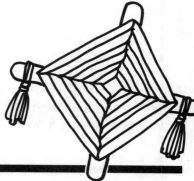

4. To change colors, knot the ends of the two pieces of yarn together and trim off any extra ends.

5. Continue to weave in one of these ways until about 1 1/2 inches (4 cm) of stick (straw) is left uncovered at the end. Add a drop of glue at the end of the last woven piece of yarn to hold it in place.

6. If desired, add tassels to the sides or bottom of the God's Eye. To make a tassel, wind the yarn around the width of a ruler 6 or 7 times.
   a. For side tassels, slip the yarn off the ruler and over the end of the stick (or straw). Tie it in place with another piece of yarn and then add glue to prevent it from slipping off. Cut open the bottom loops and trim any uneven pieces.
   b. For a bottom tassel, slip the yarn off the ruler onto another piece of yarn. With a separate piece of yarn, tie the yarn together near the top and cut open the bottom loops. Tie the tassel onto the bottom of the God's Eye Weaving.

7. The weavings can be hung by thread at the top. Or roll up pieces of masking tape and stick them onto the back of the ornament. Press the God's Eye onto a wall or bulletin board for display.

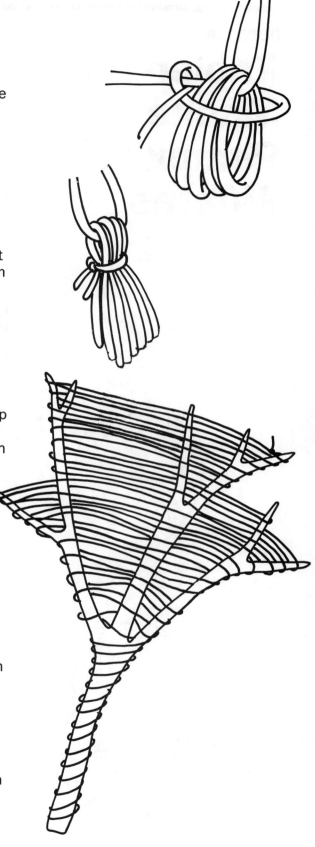

Twisted Twig Weavings

1. Try weaving with branches as looms. Choose twigs that have many shoots that twist and branch out. Use different colors of yarn to weave under and over, around and through the branching parts. For example, loop from a thicker, lower shoot way up to a tiny shoot, leaving a large open space between. Then extend the yarn down and create a number of tightly woven rows in a forked area where two parts of the branch meet.

2. Students can design and create beautiful weavings from these natural looms. Hang the weavings with yarn.

Papier-Mâché Pumpkin Piñatas

What You Need

round 9-inch (23-cm) balloons

flour and water

mixing bowl

spoon

newspaper

sharp knife *for teacher*

scissors *for teacher*

heavy string

tempera and paintbrushes

small wrapped goodies to fill piñata (dried fruit, candies, toys)

masking tape

stick (to hit piñata)

Safety Note: Teacher or another adult should blow up balloons and cut hardened papier-mâché.

What You Do

1. Piñatas are colorful papier-mâché decorations used for celebrations in Mexico and other places. They're filled with candies, small toys, and other gifts. Piñatas are hung and children take turns hitting them with a stick to release the goodies inside. Celebrate this Halloween by creating a Pumpkin Piñata.

2. Remind students that papier-mâché is a method of building up layers of paper strips soaked in a paste-water solution to create objects. It's easy to mold and is strong when it dries.

3. A teacher or another adult should blow up the balloons and knot the ends.

4. Students can work in pairs to cover one balloon with papier-mâché, or each student can work on his or her own. Mix 3 cups (.71 liters) flour and 3 3/4 cups (925 ml) water in a bowl to make a smooth, slightly runny paste. This amount will cover one 9-inch (23-cm) balloon with four layers of newspaper. If necessary, mix more paste using the proportion of 2 cups (500 ml) flour to 2 1/2 cups (.60 liters) water, but don't use more than four layers of newspaper.

5. Tear newspaper sheets into strips about 1 1/2 inch x 3 inches (4 cm x 8 cm). Dip a strip in the bowl and then drag it through the flour-water mixture, rubbing off the excess as it is pulled out over the rim of the bowl.

6. Place the soaked paper strip on the balloon and press it down. Add soaked strips, one by one, slightly overlapping one another, all around the balloon until it is completely covered. Leave a small area right around the knot of the balloon (and the knot itself) uncovered. To make the piñata stronger, build up three more layers of strips around the balloon.

7. Let the balloon dry thoroughly (for about a week). Turn it each day so that it dries on all sides.

8. When the piñata is dry and hard, the teacher or another adult should use a knife to cut a hole about 2 1/2 inches (6 cm) in diameter at the knotted end. Pop and remove the balloon. The teacher should then turn the piñata over and use the sharp ends of a scissors to poke two small holes about 2 inches (5 cm) apart from each other in the top.

9. Students should insert a long length of string through the two small holes, reaching inside the big hole to push the string through.

10. Paint the piñata with bright colors of tempera to create a unique pumpkin face. Allow the paint to dry.

11. Insert small *wrapped* dried fruit, candy, toys, and other little gifts through the opening. Tear masking tape strips and neatly tape over the hole until it is sealed. Hang the piñata from the string.

12. Students can take turns hitting the Papier-Mâché Pumpkin Piñatas with a stick until the tape breaks and the Halloween treats come tumbling out of the hole. The unbroken Pumpkin Piñatas may be left as hanging decorations.

Stuffed Scarecrow

What You Need

For each student:

newspaper (to work on and for stuffing)

large brown paper bag

crayons, markers, or tempera and paintbrushes

old worn-out clothes (long-sleeved shirt, pants, hat)

straw (optional)

string

long stick, about 4 feet (1.2 m) long

What You Do

1. If possible, do this project outdoors in the schoolyard. If it's done indoors, move the desks to create a large open area of floor space. Spread newspapers or tarps on the floor. Arrange the area with piles of material in different sections: large brown paper bags, sticks, newspaper, old clothes, straw, string, art supplies (crayons, markers, tempera and paintbrushes).

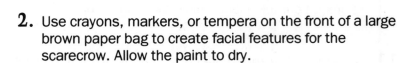

2. Use crayons, markers, or tempera on the front of a large brown paper bag to create facial features for the scarecrow. Allow the paint to dry.

3. Stuff a worn-out, long-sleeved shirt with crumpled-up pieces of newspaper. Fill the sleeves, too. If straw is available, stuff it into the ends of the sleeves so it sticks out. Tie the ends of the sleeves securely with string.

4. Insert a long stick up into the back center part of the shirt. This will serve as the body support for the scarecrow. Leave a length of the stick above the shirt so that the head may later be attached.

5. Stuff wadded newspaper into a pair of worn-out pants until they're filled. Insert the bottom end of the stick into one leg. Tie the pants securely with string over the stick around the waist. Stuff straw through the bottom of the pant legs so that it sticks out through the legs and tie the bottoms securely with string.

6. Crumple newspaper pieces to stuff the scarecrow's bag head until it is filled. Insert the top end of the stick up through the newspaper into the back center part of the bag. Add a little straw so it sticks out below the bottom of the bag. Children can ask partners to help them tie a string around the bag and stick to create the scarecrow's neck.

7. If available, an old hat may be added to the top of the bag with straw sticking out for hair.

8. Prop the scarecrows up around the room. Children may want to take their Stuffed Scarecrows home and set them out to welcome (or scare) Halloween trick-or-treaters.

Leaf Print Loose-Leaf Scrapbook

What You Need

white fabric (size of loose-leaf cover)
loose-leaf notebook
fresh leaves
newspaper
crayons (autumn colors)
iron *for teacher*
white glue
white drawing paper
hole punch

Safety Note: Students should not go near hot iron.

What You Do

1. Children can make a leaf print scrapbook of all the different leaves they can find and identify. Use a white piece of fabric cut to the size of a loose-leaf notebook cover.

2. To make leaf prints to decorate the fabric cover, have children put fresh leaves on a sheet of newspaper with the vein sides facing up. Use different colors of crayons to color the backs (vein sides) of the leaves. Several colors might be used on one leaf to give the feeling of an autumn leaf changing colors. Each leaf should be completely colored with a thick layer of crayon. Work slowly on a small section at a time, being careful not to tear the leaf.

3. Place the fabric onto a sheet of newspaper. Place the leaf, crayon side down, onto the fabric. Cover the leaf with another sheet of newspaper.

4. A teacher or another adult should press with an iron at a medium setting to melt the crayon wax. The pattern and crayon wax will transfer from the leaf onto the fabric.

5. Children can glue the leaf-decorated fabric onto the cover of the loose-leaf notebook.

6. Individual leaf prints can be made on separate sheets of white drawing paper using the same method. Punch holes so that the pages can be inserted into the binder. Have students identify each leaf and write its name on the page, along with any information about it.

7. Children can keep adding new leaves to the Leaf Print Loose-Leaf Scrapbook during the year.

What You Need

corrugated cardboard with ribs exposed
scissors
small, serrated knife
tempera and paintbrushes
thin paper
spoon
ruler
crayon

Note: Adult supervision required for this project.

Corrugated Cardboard Prints

Halloween Cards

Corrugated cardboard is heavy paper with alternating ridges and grooves. It's used for protecting items that are wrapped in it. Corrugated cardboard can also be used for printing your own spooky Halloween cards.

What You Do

1. Begin by experimenting with a small piece of corrugated cardboard, 4 inches (10 cm) square. Place the cardboard on a flat surface. *Carefully,* use a knife to cut away some of the ribs of the cardboard. Cut across the ridges. Make some cuts deeper than others. But be careful not to cut too deep. You don't want to go through to the other side of the cardboard.

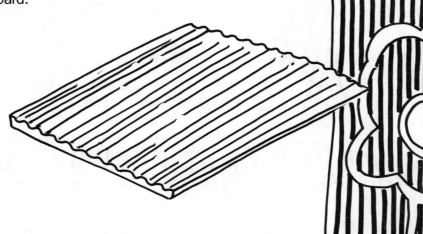

2. Using tempera, color the entire surface of the cardboard. To make a print, press a piece of paper onto the cardboard while the paint is still wet. Rub the back of the paper with the back of a spoon. Then carefully lift off the paper. You've made a corrugated print.

3. Notice the way different areas of the print look: where your cuts were deeper, where your cuts were shallower, and where there were no ridges cut away.

Printing Halloween Cards

1. Cut out a 7 inch x 9 inch (18 cm x 23 cm) piece of corrugated cardboard. Use a crayon to draw the outline of a simple Halloween shape, such as a bat, ghost, witch, or skeleton.

2. Follow the same steps that you used for your experimental card. But instead of cutting and coloring the entire card, work only within the area of the Halloween shape. Remember to cut some parts deeper than others. After you've made one kind of print, you can experiment with other sheets of corrugated cardboard and other Halloween spooks.

3. Try making Corrugated Cardboard Prints for other occasions during the year.

24

What You Need

acorns (or acorn substitutes)
container (to soak the acorns)
water
large needle and heavy nylon thread
scissors
fine-line markers

Acorn Jewelry

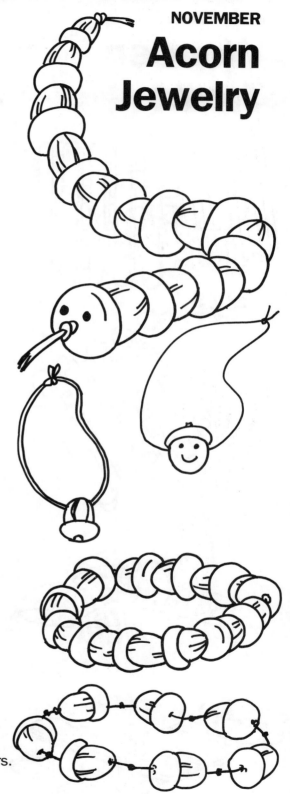

What You Do

1. If there are oak trees near the school, take a class nature walk to gather acorns from the ground. (Acorns grow in the Northeast and Midwest.) If acorns are not available in your area, create jewelry with other nuts, seeds, or beans. Try to select substitutes that can be pierced with a needle after they've been softened in water.

2. Soak acorns in water overnight to soften them for stringing. The nuts should be strung while they are soft and damp. Use a large needle to pierce the softened acorns and string them together onto heavy nylon thread.

3. Here are some ideas for acorn bracelets and necklaces:
    a. *Acorn Snake Necklace.* Start with a large acorn. Poke the needle and thread through the top center part of the acorn *cap* through the entire length of the acorn. This acorn will be the snake's head. Continue stringing acorns, progressing from the biggest in the front to the smallest at the end of the snake's body. Cut and tie the thread at the ends, making sure enough thread is used so that the tied necklace will fit over a child's head. When the acorns dry, use markers to make a snake face on the first acorn.
    b. *Acorn Face Necklace.* This time, string the acorns through the middle right below the cap. The acorn caps are "hats" that sit on acorn heads. When the acorns dry, use markers to add facial features.
    c. *Acorn Flower Necklace.* Invert the acorn so the cap is on the bottom. String the acorns through the top of the "flower" part with the cap as the petal base. Decorate the dry acorns with markers to look like flowers.
    d. *Acorn Bracelets.* Acorns may be strung together one after the other or spaced out and separated with knots.

Wooden Trivet

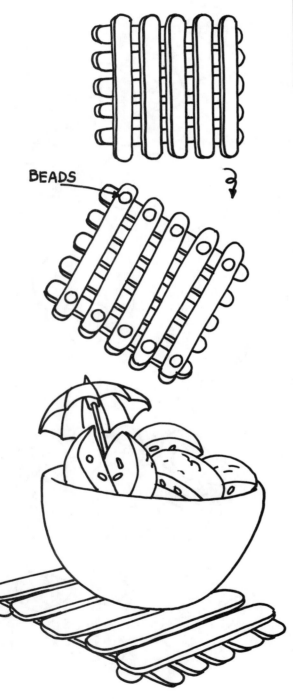

BEADS

What You Need

10 craft sticks
newspaper (to work on)
acrylic paints and paintbrushes
acrylic gloss medium and varnish and brush *for teacher*
aluminum foil
white glue
10 wooden beads

What You Do

1. Here's a ''cool'' item—a small wooden trivet for holding cold dishes that is decorative enough for students to put on their dining tables at home or to give as Thanksgiving gifts. These trivets should *never* be used for hot dishes because they're not heat resistant.

2. Paint one side of each of craft stick either one color or several colors. Allow the paint to dry completely.

3. A teacher or another adult should brush on a coat of gloss medium and varnish. When the first coat dries, add a second coat and let it dry. The gloss medium and varnish will make the sticks shine.

4. To create the trivet, arrange five of the sticks vertically, painted side up, on a piece of foil, so that there is about 1/2 inch (1 cm) of space between each one.

5. Place the other five sticks horizontally on top of the first five, allowing a little less than 1/2 inch (1 cm) of space between each stick. Try to arrange the sticks so that the ends line up evenly with one another. Glue the horizontal sticks onto the vertical ones.

6. Use the wooden beads as ''legs'' for the crossed sticks to stand on. The beads will separate the bottom of the trivet from the table surface. Glue the beads to the bottom five sticks, about 1/2 inch (1 cm) from each end.

The trivet is ready for a cool dish!

Pomander Balls

What You Need

firm orange (lemon or lime may also be used)
whole cloves
thimble (to protect finger while inserting cloves)
ground cloves, cinnamon, and nutmeg
bowl (for ground spice mixture)
pretty ribbon (or colorful yarn)

What You Do

1. Tell students that long ago, before sanitation trucks hauled off garbage, women carried fragrant balls to smell when the odors in the street became too strong. Today pomander balls add a sweet, spicy smell to closets and other places. They make great gifts for Thanksgiving.

2. To make a pomander ball, press the stems of whole cloves into a firm orange. Wear a thimble on the index finger to protect it while pressing. The cloves should be pushed into the rind as close together as possible until the whole fruit is covered with them.

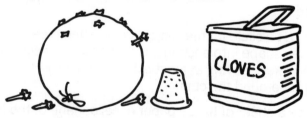

3. Make a mixture of equal parts of ground cloves, cinnamon, and nutmeg. Roll the clove-covered orange into the ground-spice mixture. Lightly tap off the excess.

4. Tie a ribbon around the pomander ball and make a loop for hanging. Add a bow or other small decoration near the top under the loop.

5. Hang the ball. It will take about two or three weeks for the fruit to shrivel, dry, and harden. The Pomander Ball's fresh fragrance and spicy aroma will fill the air.

Stained-Glass Turkey Medallions

What You Need

compass or circular plate about 8 inches (20 cm) in diameter

black construction paper

pencil

scissors

tissue paper or cellophane of different colors

white glue

What You Do

1. Tell children they will cut an openwork design within a turkey shape to create a medallion with a stained-glass look.

2. Make a circle 8 inches (20 cm) in diameter on a sheet of black construction paper. (Use a compass or plate to measure.)

3. Cut out the circle. Then draw another circle about 1/2 inch (1 cm) in from the outer circle. Using the inner circle as the edge, draw the outline of a turkey. Cut out the space between the turkey outline and the interior circle border.

4. Cut out a circle for the turkey's eye. Then break up the turkey shape into sections. Cut openwork designs within the turkey, leaving at least a 1/4-inch (1/2-cm) black border around the cuts.

5. Place a sheet of tissue paper or cellophane of the color of your choice over the circle and trace all of the cutout sections between the turkey outline and the circle border. Cut out the tissue paper (or cellophane), making the shapes slightly larger than the tracings. Do not use this color for the interior of the turkey.

6. Choose different colors of tissue paper (or cellophane) for each of the sections of the interior of the turkey.Trace over the cutout designs, and cut out the tissue paper slightly larger than the tracings.

7. Glue the tissue paper shapes to the back of the black construction paper, matching each with its corresponding spaces. Allow the glue to dry.

8. Hang the medallions in a window. Light will shine through the tissue paper, highlighting the Stained-Glass Turkey Medallions.

Thanksgiving Patchwork Quilt

What You Need

6-inch (15-cm) white paper squares
pencil
scissors
colorful, patterned scraps of fabric
6-inch (15-cm) solid-color fabric squares
needle, thread, straight pins
quilt batting
muslin
large darning or crewel needle
thin baby yarn

What You Do

1. Discuss patchwork with students. Explain that the pioneers pieced and sewed together leftover scraps of fabric or pieces from worn-out clothes to make tops for quilts. Patchwork was an economical way of using leftover pieces of cloth. Varied and beautiful patterns and designs were created. The patchwork tops were then quilted—sewn onto a backing with padding in between—to make warm blankets for winter and other functional items.

2. For Thanksgiving, ask the class to work together to create a patchwork quilt to donate to a center for the homeless, children's hospital, children's aid society, or nursing home.

3. Begin with a 6-inch (15-cm) square piece of white paper. Each student should draw a simple design of something for which he or she is thankful. Shapes might depict family figures, a house, a pet, flowers, birds, the sun, a pond, a rainbow, and so on. Cut out the overall shape. Then divide the design into several sections. For example, each flower shape might be cut into individual petals, a stem, and leaves; a rainbow into several arched bands. (*Note:* Students can design more than one square, depending on the size of the class and the size of the quilt desired.)

4. Pin the cutout pieces to colorful, patterned fabric scraps and cut them out. Arrange the fabric scraps on the solid-color 6-inch (15-cm) fabric square to re-create the overall shape. Sew the shapes onto the fabric square.

5. Those students who like to sew can cut out other scraps of fabric to add a further dimension to the design. For example, to the basic shape of a house, cut small pieces of fabric for windows, curtains, a door, a doorknob, a chimney. Sew these pieces in place on top of, or overlapping, the basic shape.

6. When the individual squares are ready, arrange them into rows of five squares (or the number of squares needed for the desired width of the quilt). Lay out the pattern for the entire quilt. The students whose squares form each row can take turns sewing the squares together to make a strip. Using small stitches, sew two squares together, front to front, along one side close to the edge. Then add the other squares to the strip.

7. Sew the strips (rows) together, front to front, along one side to make a large patchwork top for the quilt.

8. Clear a large work space on the floor. Cut out a piece of quilt batting 1 inch (2 1/2 cm) larger all around than the patchwork top and a piece of muslin 2 inches (5 cm) larger all around than the top. Place the muslin on the floor. Center the batting on the muslin. Then center the patchwork top faceup on the batting. Pin all three layers together.

9. Have a "quilting bee." A group of students can sit around the quilt and take turns at what is called "tying knots" to join the three layers together. Here's how: Thread large-eye darning or crewel needles with thin baby yarn. Do not knot the end. The teacher should demonstrate tying the first knot.

   Start in the middle of the center square at the exact center of the quilt. Put the needle *down* the square through the three layers from top to bottom (hole A). Pull the yarn through so that a 2 1/2–3 inch (6–8 cm) tail of yarn is left sticking up at the top of the quilt. About 1/8–1/4 inch (1/4–1/2 cm) from where the needle was brought down, make hole B by bringing the needle back *up* through the muslin, batting, and top layer. Then put the needle back down through hole A and up through hole B again (it's sort of like sewing a button).

   The yarn is now on top. Tie the two ends together twice to knot. Cut the yarn, leaving about 3/4 inch (2 cm) of yarn hanging on top of the square for decoration.

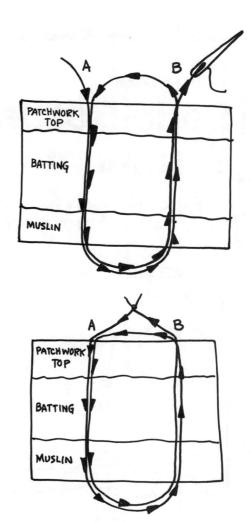

10. Students should tie the center of each square in this manner, working from the middle of the quilt out. As they knot, students should smooth the quilt so there are no puckers, tucks, or folds on the backing. Once all of the squares have been tied, the border can be sewn.

11. Those students who don't like to sew or have difficulty with it can do the pinning. They can sit around the border of the quilt. Working with one side at a time, they can turn the muslin up over the patchwork top to create a double-fold border all around the quilt. They should pin the muslin to the outside edges of the top.

12. Another group of students can stitch around the border. (Left-handed students should sit on one side so they're all sewing in the same direction.) Each student can sew a small section using either a small running or hemming stitch (decide on one type of stitch for everyone to use) until the whole border is stitched. If necessary, demonstrate the sewing stitches.

13. Take some photographs of the finished quilt and display them in the classroom. Then donate the Thanksgiving Patchwork Quilt to the needy.

Soda-Bottle Terrarium

Here's some craft magic—turning a soda bottle into a terrarium!

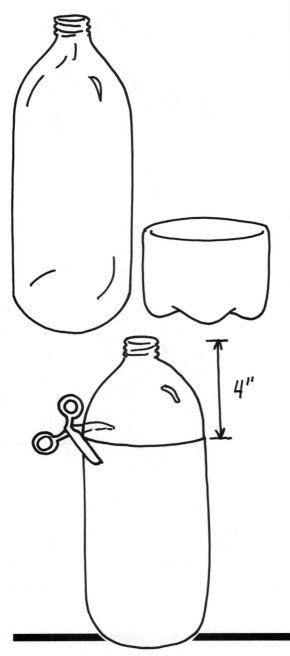

4"

What You Need

1 plastic 2-liter soda bottle with the extra "cup-type" bottom base and bottle cap

hot water

soap

tape measure

crayon

scissors

gravel

saucer

potting soil

seeds (from citrus fruit or seed packet or lima beans)

What You Do

1. The parts of the plastic soda bottle can be separated, cut, and repositioned to make a terrarium. To separate the "cup" base from the rest of the bottle, pour hot (not boiling) tap water into the bottle until it is about half full.

2. Screw on the bottle cap. Let the water stand for several minutes. This soaking will soften the glue connecting the bottle to the bottom piece. Gently pull the plastic base off the end of the bottle. If it doesn't come off easily, make the water in the bottle a little hotter. (Remember, do not use boiling water because plastic softens easily. You wouldn't want it to "get bent out of shape!")

3. Once you have removed the base, you will see the dome shape of the clear plastic bottle.

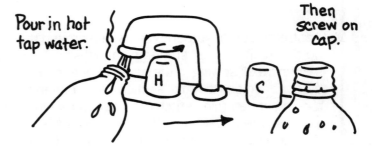

Pour in hot tap water.

Then screw on cap.

4. Pour out the water. Soak the labels off the bottle with warm water and soap. If the glue doesn't come off easily, scrub it gently with a soapy sponge. Shake out excess water from the inside of the bottle and dry the outside.

5. Measure 4 inches (10 cm) down from the bottle top and mark the spot with a crayon. Turn the bottle and mark off 4 inches (10 cm) from the top at several other points. Draw a line around the bottle at the 4-inch (10-cm) mark, connecting all the points.

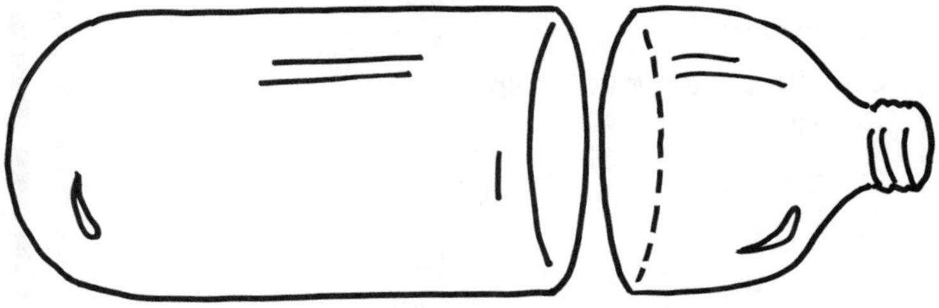

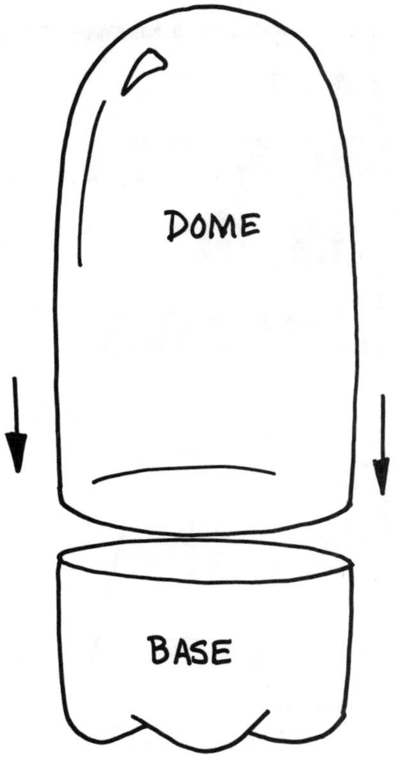

DOME

BASE

6. With the point of a sharp scissors, have an adult punch a hole in the bottle slightly above the line. Ask the adult to cut down to the crayon line for you. You or the adult can continue cutting around the bottle along the crayon line. Be careful of any sharp edges. Discard the top part of the bottle that you have cut off.

7. Turn the bottle upside down (dome side pointing up), so that the cut part sits inside the plastic base.

8. Put the base on the saucer, place some gravel at the bottom of the base, and fill it with potting soil. (You'll notice that there already are drainage holes in the base.) Plant some seeds or lima beans, water the soil, and set the dome back on the base.

9. Making Soda-Bottle Terrariums will "grow" on you!

SOIL
FOR GENERAL USE

Macaroni Mosaic Windows

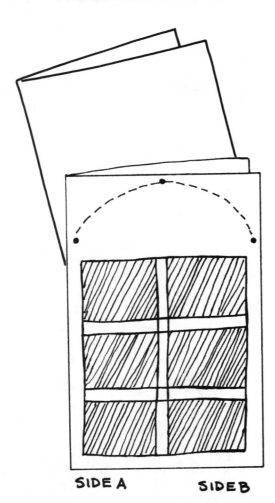

SIDE A   SIDE B

What You Need

1 cup (250 ml) raw macaroni (for each mosaic)
tempera and paintbrushes
cardboard
colorful construction paper
pencil
scissors
ruler
white glue
clear plastic wrap
transparent tape

What You Do

1. Discuss with children that a mosaic is a picture or design made by inlaying small colorful pieces, such as tiles, onto a surface. For this mosaic, they will inlay with colorful macaroni.

2. Divide the macaroni into separate piles so that there is one pile for each color of paint. Place the first pile on a corner of a sheet of cardboard and paint the macaroni. Only the surface facing up needs to be painted. Continue to add piles and paint them until all the piles are finished. Allow 15 minutes for the paint to dry.

3. To make the window frame, fold a sheet of construction paper in half vertically. Use a ruler to find the center of the paper at the top and place a dot in that spot. Then measure 1 inch (2 1/2 cm) down from the top on both the right and left sides of the paper and mark each spot with a dot.

4. Draw a semicircle to connect the three dots. Keep the paper folded and cut along the penciled line through both thicknesses of paper.

5. Draw a rectangle inside the frame, leaving about 1/2 inch (1 cm) for a border. Draw two lines down the center of the rectangle with about 1/2 inch (1 cm) of space between the lines.

6. Divide both sides A and B into 3 sections, drawing double lines about 1/4 inch (1/2 cm) apart. (The lines can be drawn either straight or wavy.) These lines are the window dividers.

7. Open the paper and cut out the centers of the sections (the shaded area in the diagram), but do not cut through the dividers. Fold the paper back to see the uncut half of the paper through the window frame.

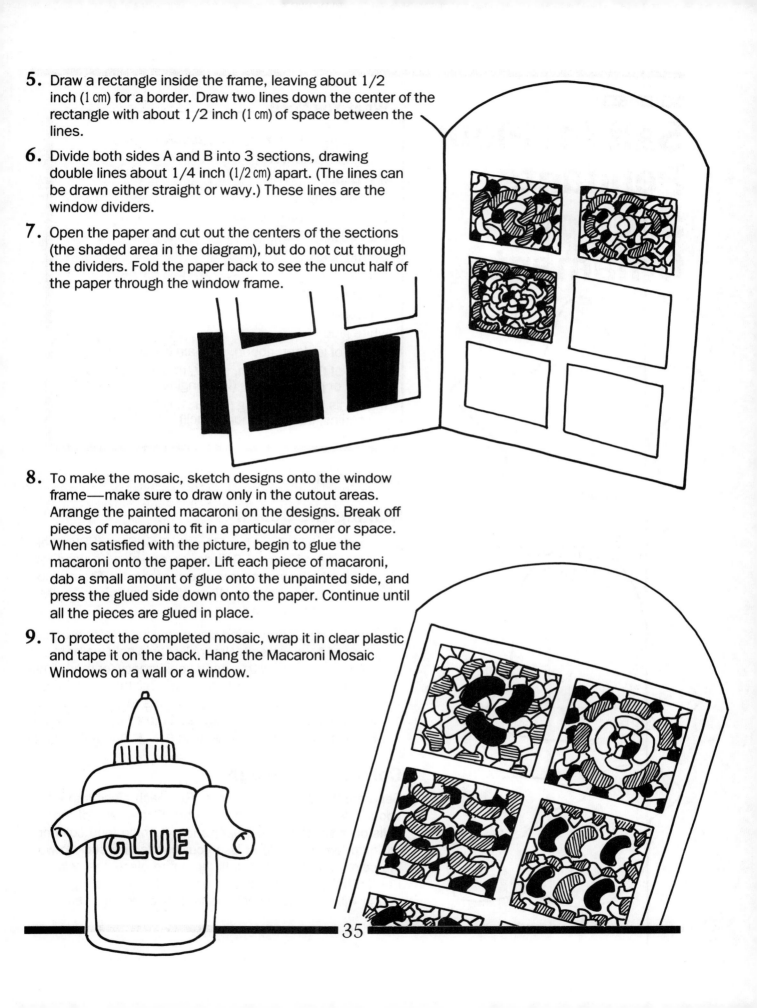

8. To make the mosaic, sketch designs onto the window frame—make sure to draw only in the cutout areas. Arrange the painted macaroni on the designs. Break off pieces of macaroni to fit in a particular corner or space. When satisfied with the picture, begin to glue the macaroni onto the paper. Lift each piece of macaroni, dab a small amount of glue onto the unpainted side, and press the glued side down onto the paper. Continue until all the pieces are glued in place.

9. To protect the completed mosaic, wrap it in clear plastic and tape it on the back. Hang the Macaroni Mosaic Windows on a wall or a window.

Salt 'n' Flour Pendants and Ornaments

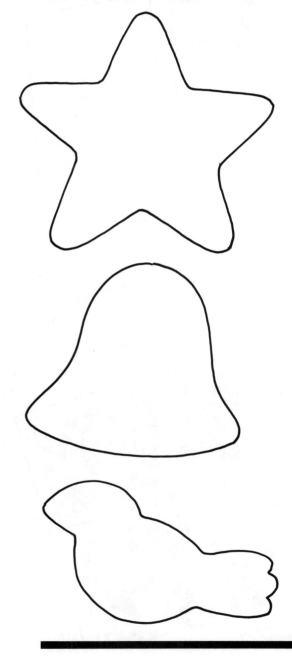

What You Need

measuring cup, mixing bowl, spoon

flour, salt, cold water

wax paper

food coloring

tempera and paintbrushes

craft stick

plastic bag

pencil

sheet of paper

scissors

white glue

pieces of leather, ribbon, or chain (for pendant)

pieces of thin wire, yarn, string, ribbon, plastic bag ties, or pipe cleaners (for hanging ornaments)

materials for decorating (glitter, tiny beads, sequins, buttons, short pencil)

What You Do

Making the Dough

1. Remind children of the Flour 'n' Salt School Supplies they made. Flour 'n' Salt dough can also be used for making holiday pendants and ornaments. There's no need to bake the clay. When the dough air-dries, the objects become hard.

2. Make the self-hardening clay by mixing together equal parts of flour and salt. Gradually stir in cold water to create a mixture with a good consistency for modeling. Knead the clay by hand. When the mixture is no longer sticky, it's ready. If the dough seems too dry, add more water. If it seems too sticky, add more flour and salt. Each student should begin with a large handful of dough.

Coloring the Dough

Separate the dough into pieces. Roll each piece into a ball about 1 ½ inches (4 cm) in diameter. Flatten one of the balls on a sheet of wax paper and put some food coloring or liquid tempera onto it. Use your hands or a stick to work the color into the dough until the entire piece has color. Put the ball into a plastic bag and seal it, so that the dough will stay soft as color is added to the other balls.

Salt 'n' Flour Pendants

1. Decide on a shape for the pendant.

2. Draw the shape onto a sheet of paper and cut it out. Flatten one of the colorful dough balls—at least 1/4 inch (1/2 cm) thick—and trace the pattern onto it. Cut out the shape using a craft stick. Use the eraser end of a pencil to make a hole near the top of the pendant. Make sure the hole goes through the entire shape.

3. Use the other colors of dough to decorate the shape. Small dough beads or wormlike shapes can be added to the surface of the pendant shape. Use glue to stick each piece of dough onto the pendant. Let the pendant dry thoroughly.

4. Slip a length of leather, a ribbon, or chain through the hole at the top of the pendant so that it can be worn.

Salt 'n' Flour Ornaments

Students should use their imaginations to create holiday ornaments for hanging on a Christmas tree, standing at the tree base, or propping on a table next to a menorah. Begin with a 1 ½ inch (4 cm) ball of clay for each ornament. Ornaments should be at least ¼ inch (½ cm) thick. Insert a pencil hole in the top of the ornaments for hanging. Dry the finished objects by placing them flat to harden, and then hang them to complete the drying process. Insert thin wire, yarn, string, ribbon, plastic bag ties, or pipe cleaners into the holes for hanging. Create Santas, angels, elves, gingerbread people, etc. Here are some ideas.

Candy Cane

1. Use red and white dough. Put a red clay ball on a sheet of wax paper on a flat surface. Move the fingertips of both hands back and forth until the clay is rolled into a snakelike shape. Keep the movements even and smooth. If the snake breaks, stick it back together and roll it again. Roll out a piece of white dough into a snake shape of the same size.

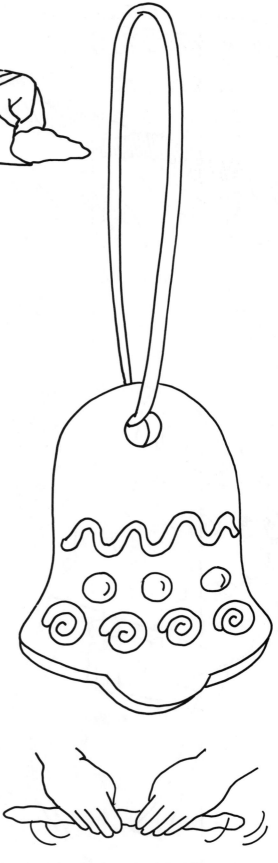

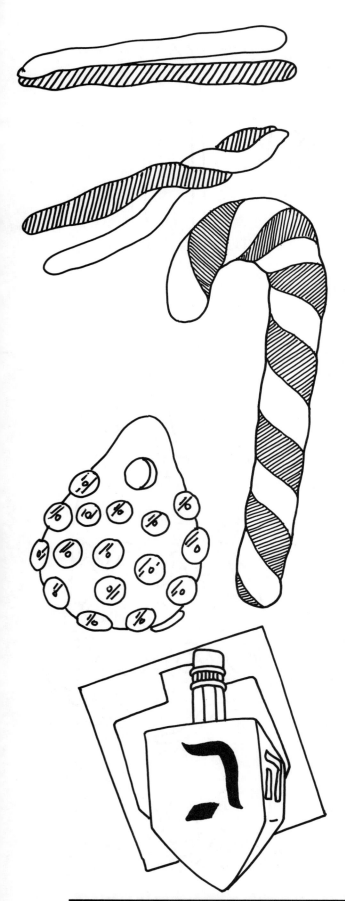

2. Place the two snake pieces next to each other. Pinch the red and white pieces together at one end and gently twist them together to make "stripes." Gently roll the twisted shape against the flat surface to make it smooth. Curve one end into a hook for the candy cane.

Stocking

1. Flatten a clay ball and cut out the shape of a Christmas stocking using a craft stick. Roll out tiny stringlike pieces of different colors of dough and shape them into the letters of someone's name or initials. Glue the letters onto the front of the stocking, running down from top to bottom.

2. Roll the clay into little balls and flatten into leaf shapes to decorate the cuff of the stocking with red holly berries and green leaves. Or press out some small flat clay circles to make a teddy bear shape and glue it onto the stocking. Or decorate the stocking by pressing buttons into the clay to make imprints. (The button imprints can be painted with tempera when the clay dries.)

Christmas Ball

Roll the clay into a ball. Pinch the ball at the top to make a sort of teardrop shape. Spread one side of the ball with glue and sprinkle it with red and green glitter. Cover the rest of the ball that way. Or try rolling a glue-covered ball in a pile of tiny colorful beads. Or glue on sequins to cover the ball. Make a pencil hole through the clay just below the pinched part for hanging.

Dreidel

A dreidel is a spinning top with a Hebrew letter on each side. To make a dreidel for Hanukkah, press a clay ball into somewhat of a cube shape by flattening each "side" with the palms of your hands. Insert a short pencil completely through the top and bottom squares so that it sticks out at both ends with the point on the bottom. Pinch the clay at the bottom of the dreidel so it looks like a top. Roll stringlike pieces of different colors of clay to form a Hebrew letter on each square of the dreidel. Glue the letters onto the clay. Here's what the letters look like:

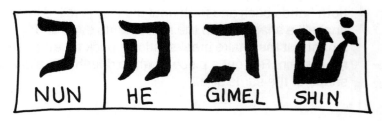

Holiday Gifts For the Birds

Popcorn-Cranberry Garlands and Pine Cone and Citrus Fruit Feeders

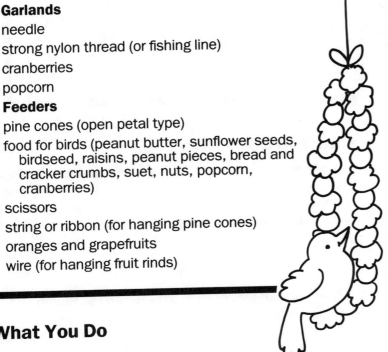

What You Need

Garlands
needle
strong nylon thread (or fishing line)
cranberries
popcorn

Feeders
pine cones (open petal type)
food for birds (peanut butter, sunflower seeds, birdseed, raisins, peanut pieces, bread and cracker crumbs, suet, nuts, popcorn, cranberries)
scissors
string or ribbon (for hanging pine cones)
oranges and grapefruits
wire (for hanging fruit rinds)

What You Do

Popcorn-Cranberry Garlands

1. Explain that garlands are wreaths or long strips made of flowers, leaves, vines, or similar materials that are used for decoration. Popcorn-Cranberry Garlands can be strung on Christmas trees. They can also be strung outside to provide food for hungry birds.

2. To make the garlands, thread a needle with a long length of strong nylon thread or fishing line. Insert the thread into a cranberry. Make a loop and large knot at the end to hold the cranberry in place. String popcorn and cranberries alternately onto the thread, sliding them down right next to one another. Continue stringing until the entire garland is filled.

3. A teacher or other adult can hang the Popcorn-Cranberry Garlands outside the school on the branch of a nearby tree.

Pine Cone and Citrus Fruit Feeders

1. Fill the openings between pine cone petals with food birds like to eat. Spread a thick layer of peanut butter on the petals and inside. Insert sunflower seeds, birdseed, raisins, peanut pieces, bread and cracker crumbs, and bits of suet into the petals.

2. Wrap string or ribbon around the cones for hanging. A teacher or other adult can tie the Pine Cone Feeders to tree branches. Or put the cones outside on a windowsill.

3. Scoop out oranges and grapefruits and fill the rinds with birdseed, nuts, peanut butter, popcorn, cranberries, and suet. Insert holes in the rinds and attach wire handles. A teacher or other adult can hang the Citrus Fruit Feeders from tree branches.

Finger Weaving: Holiday Garlands

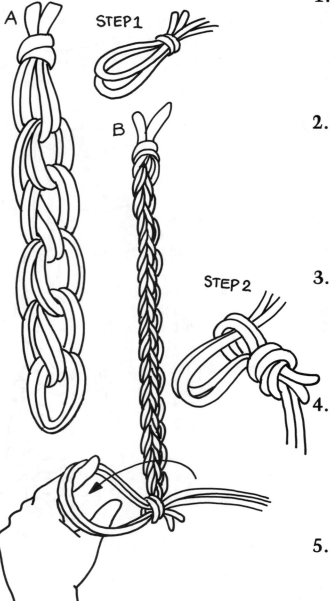

What You Need

2 colors of yarn or cord (red and green for Christmas; blue and white for Hanukkah), 4 to 5 yards (3 2/3 to 4 1/2 m) of each color for each child

scissors

ruler

What You Do

1. Hold the two strands of yarn (or cord) together and make a slip knot at one end. Leave a loop loose enough so that you'll be able to fit the tips of the thumb and index fingers of one hand through it—about 1 1/4 to 1 1/2 inches (3 to 4 cm).

2. Rest the two longer strands between the thumb and index finger of one hand. Then with the thumb and index fingers of the free hand, bring the long length of the two strands of yarn up through the loop. Pull down to make another loop about the same size as the first loop. Loops may be left large for a loose chain effect (A). Or pull the loop down to form a tight, close-knit weave (B).

3. Continue finger weaving by inserting the two strands of yarn up through the newly formed loop and pulling down to create another loop. Keep making loops until about 4 inches (10 cm) of yarn are left. Insert the unwoven ends through the last loop and pull tight.

4. Groups of children can tie their finger-woven lengths of yarn together. Make the knots right next to the woven part and cut off the unwoven ends. Create one long garland or many smaller ones. String the Finger-Woven Holiday Garlands around the room, or use them to decorate a Christmas tree.

5. Children may want to finger weave wrist or ankle bracelets, belts, or bolo ties for themselves or for holiday gifts.

What You Need

talc-free self-hardening clay

pencil

3 strands of twine—16 inches (40 cm), 14 inches (35 cm), and 12 inches (30 cm) long

3 pieces of string, 6 inches (15 cm) long

tempera and paintbrushes

Clay Bells

Ring in the holiday season with your own clay bells.

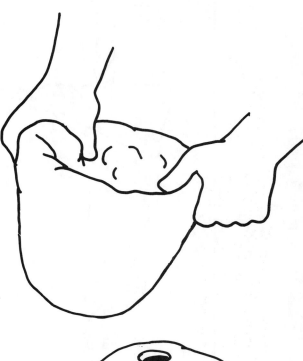

What You Do

1. To make a bell, roll a handful of clay into a ball. Press your thumb down into the center, almost to the bottom.

2. Pinch the clay together with your thumb and index finger while turning the ball around and around, until it looks like a cup. Try to make the walls of the cup even in thickness. If the clay gets too dry, wet your fingers a little to smooth and soften it.

3. Turn the cup shape over and push a pencil point into the center to make a hole. This is your first bell. Make two more bells, using less clay for each one, so that your bells are three different sizes.

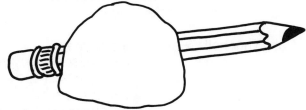

4. To make the clappers, flatten out a small ball of clay until it is very thin. Cut out a triangular shape. Make a hole near one angle. This is your first clapper. Now make two more.

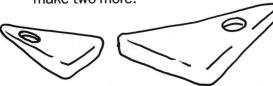

41

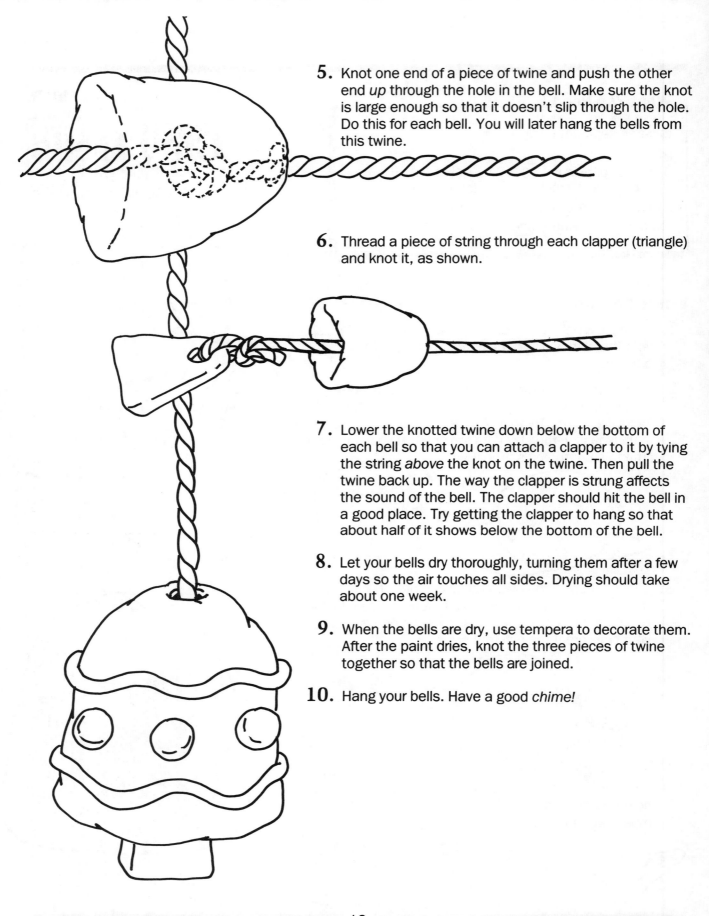

5. Knot one end of a piece of twine and push the other end *up* through the hole in the bell. Make sure the knot is large enough so that it doesn't slip through the hole. Do this for each bell. You will later hang the bells from this twine.

6. Thread a piece of string through each clapper (triangle) and knot it, as shown.

7. Lower the knotted twine down below the bottom of each bell so that you can attach a clapper to it by tying the string *above* the knot on the twine. Then pull the twine back up. The way the clapper is strung affects the sound of the bell. The clapper should hit the bell in a good place. Try getting the clapper to hang so that about half of it shows below the bottom of the bell.

8. Let your bells dry thoroughly, turning them after a few days so the air touches all sides. Drying should take about one week.

9. When the bells are dry, use tempera to decorate them. After the paint dries, knot the three pieces of twine together so that the bells are joined.

10. Hang your bells. Have a good *chime!*

What You Need

piece of burlap, 12 inches x 18 inches (30 cm x 45 cm)
tape measure
straight pins
needle and cotton thread (same color as burlap)
scissors
pieces of yarn, rope, string
white glue
paper towel tube (or similar cardboard tube)
narrow ribbon, 20 inches (50 cm) long

Burlap Wall Hanging

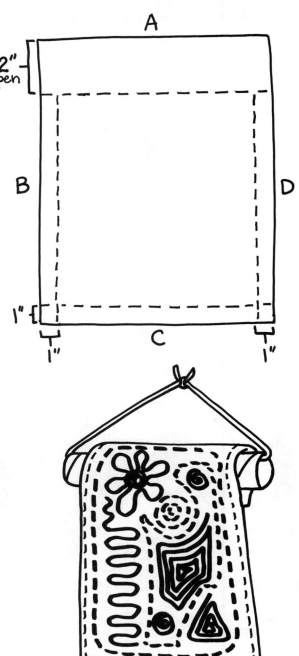

What You Do

1. Tell students that scraps of yarn, rope, and string can be recycled into an attractive wall hanging. Burlap is a coarse and durable fabric that makes an excellent background material.

2. To prevent unraveling, hem the fabric. On the three sides of the burlap, marked B, C, and D in the diagram, fold over about 1 inch (2 1/2 cm) and secure with straight pins. Sew a hem around the three sides. On the fourth side, marked A, fold over about 2 inches (5 cm), pin, and hem the edge, leaving an opening across from sides B to D. Remove all pins.

3. Create a design with the yarn, rope, and string. Make designs by twisting and winding the yarn. Dab some glue onto the yarn and stick it to the burlap.

4. Continue adding more yarn, rope, and string until the area is covered. By mixing the colors, weights, shapes, and sizes of various pieces, students can create a hanging that is interesting to the touch and appealing to the eye.

5. Allow the glue to dry for at least two hours. Put the paper towel tube through the 2-inch (5-cm) hem (Side A). Pull the ribbon through the tube and knot the ends together. The Burlap Wall Hanging is ready to be hung.

6. Burlap wall hangings can also be created using scraps of fabric.

Inside-Outside Snow Mobile

What You Need

construction paper (different colors)
pencil
scissors
ruler
thread
newspaper (to work on)
white glue
crayons or markers
wire coat hanger
white ribbon (to cover hanger frame)

What You Do

1. Explain that a mobile is a sculpture that moves, with parts that are made from paper, wood, or other materials. The movable parts hang down from wire or string, arranged so that they balance and can float freely in space. Tell students they will create a paper mobile with a snowy or wintery theme. A single thread will join two separate pieces that will turn and float freely, one inside the other.

2. Encourage students to visualize ''inside-outside'' ideas for their ''snow'' mobiles.

3. Follow the basic guidelines given for a skater on a pond to create any inside-outside mobiles. Make a drawing of the pond on a sheet of construction paper. Place a second sheet of the same color paper underneath and cut out both pieces together to make a matched set. Draw the ice skater on a different-color paper, back it with another sheet, and cut out the pair. Remember, the ice-skater must be made an appropriate size to ''fit'' in the outer pond piece. Cut out the center of the pond piece just large enough for the ice skater to fit in it.

4. Measure a length of thread three times as long as the pond. Put one drawing of the pond facedown on a sheet of newspaper. Center one picture of the skater in the pond. Place the thread along the center vertically and glue it from the bottom of the pond, over the skater, to the top of the pond. A loose length of thread should extend off the paper. Let the glue dry. Cut a hole in top of triangle.

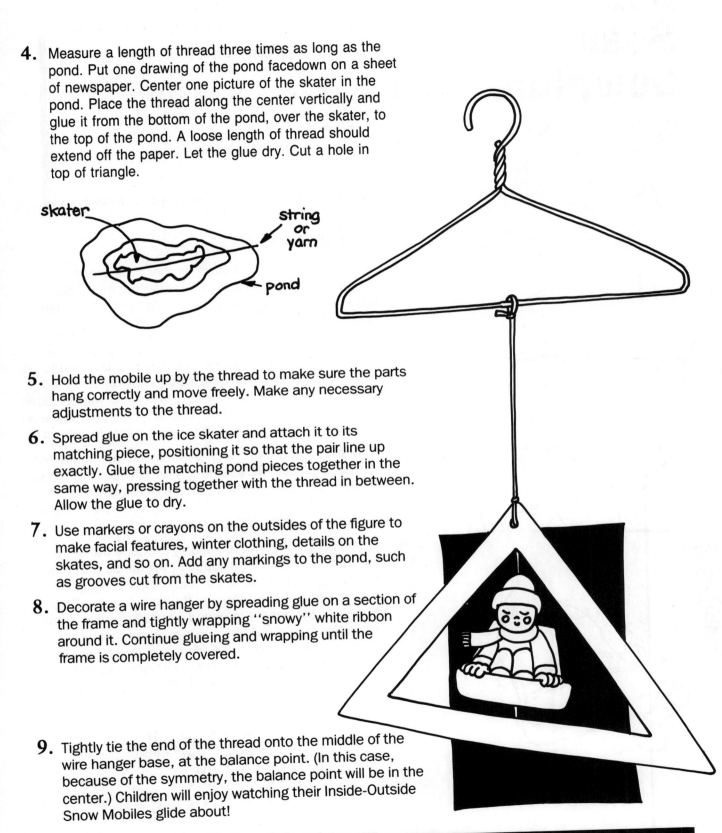

skater

string or yarn

pond

5. Hold the mobile up by the thread to make sure the parts hang correctly and move freely. Make any necessary adjustments to the thread.

6. Spread glue on the ice skater and attach it to its matching piece, positioning it so that the pair line up exactly. Glue the matching pond pieces together in the same way, pressing together with the thread in between. Allow the glue to dry.

7. Use markers or crayons on the outsides of the figure to make facial features, winter clothing, details on the skates, and so on. Add any markings to the pond, such as grooves cut from the skates.

8. Decorate a wire hanger by spreading glue on a section of the frame and tightly wrapping ''snowy'' white ribbon around it. Continue glueing and wrapping until the frame is completely covered.

9. Tightly tie the end of the thread onto the middle of the wire hanger base, at the balance point. (In this case, because of the symmetry, the balance point will be in the center.) Children will enjoy watching their Inside-Outside Snow Mobiles glide about!

Soap Sculpture

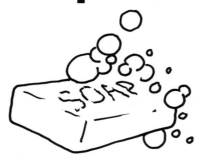

What You Need

large rectangular bar of white soap
sheet of paper
table knife or paring knife (not too sharp)
metal nail file
empty tin can
piece of fabric (to drape over can)
scissors

Note: Adult supervision required for this project.

What You Do

1. Discuss sculpture as a three-dimensional design. Sculptures are made from many different materials. An especially good material is soap. It's inexpensive, firm, and fun to carve using only a few tools.

2. Encourage students to look at the soap bar and to use their imaginations to decide what they would like it to be: a face, an animal, a building. Depending on their geographic location, children might think of wintery ideas such as a snowman, a sled, and ice skates, or maybe an ice-cream cone or surfboard! Choose a simple subject.

3. Work over a sheet of paper to catch and later reuse the carved-off pieces. Scrape off any letters from the brand name of the soap in order to begin with a smooth surface. Draw the outline of the subject on the surface of the soap with the point of a nail file.

4. Use a paring knife (not too sharp) to shape the soap. Tell students to hold the soap in their hands with their thumbs against the soap bar and their other fingers wrapped around the soap and the knife handle. They should cut the soap *slowly* and *carefully* toward them. Cut shavings or small bits and pieces from the soap. Do a little at a time. Keep the knife clean. Brush the shavings from the sculpture every so often so they don't stick to it. Use the point of a nail file to add fine lines or details.

5. Tell students to turn the soap often as they work, explaining that a sculpture is seen not just from the front, but from all sides. By turning the soap and working on all areas, the finished sculpture will look as good from one angle as another.

6. Remember to keep the design simple and try to retain some of the shape of the original bar. Leave a flat surface on the bottom so that the carving can stand firmly and not topple over. Very gently, use fingers to smooth the finished soap sculpture.

7. Explain that a piece of sculpture is often displayed on a pedestal, or base. Find a tin can that is the right size for the finished soap sculpture: perhaps a short can, such as one from tuna fish, or a taller, larger one, as from fruit juice. Drape a piece of fabric over the entire can and cut the material to a length that covers the can.

8. Place the Soap Sculpture on top of the pedestal for display. Walk around it to see how it looks from different angles.

9. Other Ideas: Make a class Soap Sculpture Zoo by carving each bar into a different animal shape. Or shape soap into fish for a Soap Sculpture Aquarium.

To recycle the soap shavings, save them for making Ropes of Soap (see p. 58).

Chinese New Year Paper Lanterns

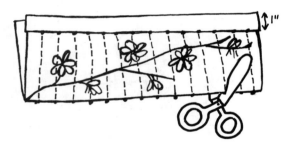

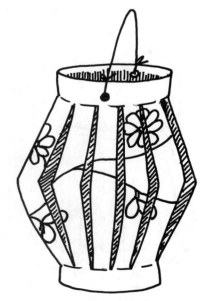

What You Need

construction paper (different colors)
ruler
pencil
crayons
scissors
white glue
string

What You Do

1. Chinese New Year is celebrated midwinter, sometime between January 21 and February 19. The celebration is marked with parades of dancing dragons and other festivities. Students can create colorful paper lanterns and then string them around the classroom to celebrate the Chinese New Year.

2. To construct a lantern, fold a sheet of construction paper in half lengthwise. Draw a 1-inch (2 1/2-cm) margin along the unfolded edge.

3. Use crayons to create a colorful design or drawing on the front and back of the paper in the space between the fold and margin. On the *back* of the paper, the folded edge will be the *top* of the drawing. (Note: the drawings will be cut into when the slits are made, but the effect will remain.)

4. Some children might like to decorate their lanterns with drawings of plum blossoms, the national flower of China that symbolizes the winter season. Explain that in China, the beautiful plum blossoms emerge and burst through the ground, unhindered by frost and snow.

5. To create slits for the lantern, make a pencil dot every 1/2 inch (1 cm) along the fold line and then along the margin line. Connect the dots. Cut slits along the lines through the folded edge up to but not through the margin.

6. Unfold the paper, curve the lantern into a cylinder, and glue it together. Let the glue dry. Use a pencil point to punch two small holes opposite each other at the top in the margin area. Insert the ends of a piece of string through the holes, from the outside to the inside, and knot the ends inside the lantern. String the lanterns around the room.

Chinese New Year Rice Paintings

What You Need

2 cups (500 ml) raw rice (for each painting)
small bowl
food coloring
spoon
paper towels
drawing paper or cardboard
pencil
white glue
clear plastic wrap (to cover painting)
tape

What You Do

1. Tell students that they can celebrate the Chinese New Year by making a rice painting of a fiery dragon. Or they can try a panda bear and bamboo, or other subject matter.

2. First prepare the rice. Put a handful of rice into a bowl. Mix in about 15 drops of food coloring. Place the dyed rice onto a paper towel.

3. Continue doing this until all the rice is dyed. When changing colors, rinse out the bowl and place each new color in a separate pile on a paper towel. To get an even greater variety of colors, mix drops of yellow and red to make orange, and so forth. Allow the rice to dry completely.

4. Draw a fiery dragon (or other picture or design) on a sheet of drawing paper or on cardboard. ''Paint'' the dragon by glueing the prepared rice onto it. First decide what colors to use in each area. Then dab a small amount of glue on the areas to be a certain color and sprinkle some rice of that color on the glue.

5. When all of the areas of the dragon are covered with rice, allow the glue to dry for about 15 minutes. When it's dry, tip the painting over a paper towel to get rid of any excess rice.

6. Wrap a piece of clear plastic around the fiery dragon and tape the plastic to the back of the paper or cardboard.

7. Children can decorate objects with rice of various colors for different occasions. They might cover a tissue box or cigar box with rice patterns.

Coiled Candleholder

Coil building is one way to make pottery. This method consists of placing coils on top of one another to create an object. Here's a coiled holder you can "hold a candle to."

What You Need

wax paper
talc-free self-hardening clay
pencil
pointed stick
tempera and paintbrushes
candle
tape

What You Do

1. Work on wax paper taped to a smooth, flat surface. To make the base for the candleholder, take a large handful of clay and press it out with your palms. Then shape it into a sort of pancake of even thickness, about 1/2 inch (1 cm) thick. The bottom must be sturdy and rest evenly on the working surface, for it is the foundation on which the candleholder will sit.

2. Make a coil by gently rolling a "log" of clay against your working surface. Move your hands back and forth several times, gently and evenly. Roll the clay with your fingers, not under your palms. Make the coil about as thick as a crayon. It's important to keep the coil the same thickness along its entire length. Roll out more coils as needed.

3. Plan the circumference of the coiled part of your candleholder. Since clay shrinks when it dries, make the width of the coiled part slightly larger than the width of the candle. Draw a faint circle with a pencil point on the top of the "pancake" base. Place the coil along the outline of this circle.

4. Before you attach the coil to the base (and later as you add other coils), make small scratches on the bottom of the coil with a pointed stick. The rough surfaces are easier to join together. Press the coil onto the base. With dampened fingers, smooth the side of the coil to the base.

5. Attach a new coil to the end of the one you have just wrapped as shown. With dampened fingers, smooth the joints together.

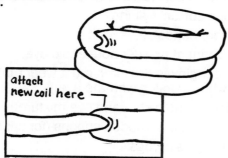

attach new coil here

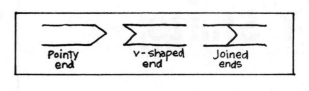

Pointy end   v-shaped end   Joined ends

6. Continue winding coils evenly around and around to build up the sides of the candleholder. Moisten your fingers as you wind the coils. Smooth the outside of the coils so they stick together as you wrap. Press them carefully and gently so that you don't change the shape.

7. Keep the coiled part straight and even by placing each coiled layer directly on top of the layer below it. By keeping the layers from overlapping one another, the candleholder will be the same width throughout. Add coils until the holder is as high as you want, being careful not to make the candleholder top-heavy.

8. Let the candleholder dry completely. Then brighten the holder by decorating it with tempera. Insert the candle. "Let there be light!"

9. Another idea is to coil a holder onto a freeform instead of a circular base.

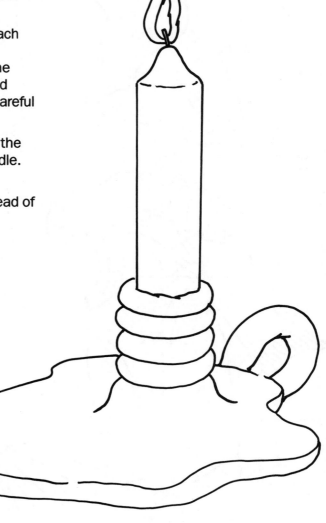

51

Tie-Dye T-Shirts

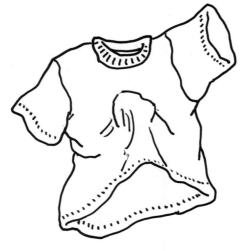

What You Need

white cotton T-shirts

rubber bands

permanent powder household dye

rubber gloves (Children must wear rubber gloves when working with the dye.)

basin (to hold shirt and dye mixture)

long-handled wooden spoons (for stirring)

old towels or rags

drying rack or clothesline

What You Do

1. Do your students each have "a shirt fit to be tied"? Explain that tie-dye is a special type of fabric dyeing. Certain sections of fabric are bound or tied before the fabric is dyed. When the fabric is put into the dye bath, the dye cannot get into the section of fabric beneath the tie. This creates interesting designs on the fabric.

2. Children should think about how the shirt will be designed. They will bind the areas they don't want covered with dye. Here's an idea to get them started. Pinch up a section of fabric from the middle front part of the shirt. Secure it tightly with a rubber band. Add three more rubber bands along that section of the fabric.

3. Bind other areas of fabric. For example, gather up a section from the sleeves, the back, and the sides, and bind them tightly with a rubber band. Add one or two more rubber bands along each section of the fabric that is to be bound. When the fabric is dyed, the bound part stays white and makes a pattern against the dyed part of the shirt.

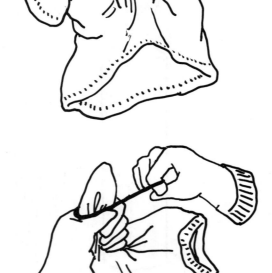

DYE

4. Before dyeing, wet the entire shirt in hot water until it is thoroughly soaked. (Rubber gloves *must* be worn when working with the dye.) Prepare the dye bath according to the package directions for hand dyeing.

5. Place the shirt in the dye bath. Make sure there is enough room in the basin for the shirt to be moved around so that the color soaks in evenly. Stir the shirt constantly with a long-handled wooden spoon. Lift the shirt up and down and turn it back and forth. Don't let it soak.

6. After about thirty minutes, put the shirt into the sink and rinse it thoroughly with warm, then cooler water, until the water runs clear. Gently squeeze the shirt, wrap it in a towel or rag to get rid of the excess water, and drape it over a drying rack or clothesline. (Clean the sink or basin.)

7. After an hour or two, remove the rubber bands from the shirt. The shirt will have circular shapes. Each design will be a surprise and will look a little different from the other designs. When all of the rubber bands are removed, drape the shirt over the rack or line again and let it dry completely.

Tie-Dye Heart Mobile

What You Need

white cotton cloth, 1 foot x 1 foot (30 cm x 30 cm)

rubber bands

red household dye or red food coloring or beet juice (see item 3 below)

measuring cup and measuring spoon

small bowl (for dyeing cloth)

rubber gloves (Children must wear rubber gloves when working with dye.)

long-handled wooden spoons (for stirring)

hot plate or stove (for *teacher* to heat beet juice)

wire clothes hanger

white glue

decorative red ribbon or red cord (to cover hanger frame and for hanging tye-dye heart)

sheet of paper, pencil, scissors

straight pins, needle, red thread

torn nylon stockings or other material for stuffing tie-dye heart

drying rack or clothesline

What You Do

1. Tell students they'll be making a valentine mobile—a stuffed tie-dye heart suspended inside a heart-shaped frame.

2. Tightly tie the cloth with rubber bands. Use three bands for each tie. (See directions for tying on page 52.)

3. Soak the tied cloth in hot water for a few minutes. Prepare any one of the following dye baths:
   a. Use a box of red household dye. Prepare dye by following package directions for hand dyeing. (If using household dye, wear rubber gloves at all times.)
   b. Mix 1 teaspoon (4 ml) red food coloring with 1 cup (250 ml) hot water.
   c. Make a natural vegetable dye from beets. The teacher or other adult heats 1 cup (250 ml) beet juice in a small pot or pan until hot. (Beet dye will turn cloth light red.)

4. Choose a bowl large enough to allow the cloth to be completely covered with dye. Soak the tied cloth in the hot dye for 20 to 30 minutes, stirring often with a spoon.

5. Remove the cloth from the dye. Do not rinse it if food coloring or beet juice was used as the dye. If household dye was used, rinse the cloth thoroughly until the water runs clear. Drape the cloth over a rack or a line to dry. After a few hours, remove the rubber bands to see the designs. Then hang the cloth to dry completely.

6. Now shape and decorate a wire hanger. Without untwisting the hook top, bend the hanger into a big heart shape. Starting at the top, spread white glue on a section of the wire frame and tightly wrap red ribbon or cord around its entire edge. Continue glueing and wrapping until the frame is completely covered.

7. When the tie-dyed cloth is dry, draw a large heart on a piece of 6 inch x 6 inch (15 cm x 15 cm) paper. Cut out the heart pattern. Fold the cloth in half and pin the paper pattern to the cloth. Cut out the heart shape and remove the pattern.

8. Use a needle and red thread to sew along the edges of the cloth, leaving an opening at the top for stuffing. Stuff the heart with torn nylon stockings or other soft material (such as facial tissues).

9. Insert about 1 1/2 inches (4 cm) of a length of red ribbon or cord (the same as used to wrap the wire frame) through the opening at the top of the heart. Sew the rest of the heart closed—sewing across the ribbon piece so that it lays flat within the heart and extends up from the top. Tack the ribbon with extra stitches, if necessary, to hold it in place.

10. Extend the length of ribbon (or cord) up to the top of the hanger just under the base of the hook. Adjust the length of the ribbon so that the heart will hang in the center within the heart frame. Cut the ribbon to the desired length and tie it onto the top of the hanger.

11. Hang the Tie-Dye Heart Mobile from the hanger hook.

Stenciled Spatter-Painted Valentine's Day Cards

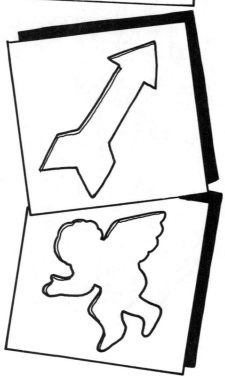

What You Need

cardboard, oaktag, or heavy paper (for stencils)

pencil

scissors

scrap paper

tempera

tray or dish (to hold paint)

craft stick

old toothbrush

piece of wire screening (optional)

drawing or construction paper (white or a color for cards)

crayons, markers, or pens (for writing message)

What You Do

Making the Stencil

1. Explain that a stencil is a sheet of paper or other thin sheet in which a design or pattern is cut. When paint is applied, it goes through the opening and the design is transferred onto another surface.

2. To make a heart stencil, first draw the heart shape on cardboard, oaktag, or heavy paper. Then cut out the heart. The frame is the stencil.

3. Make heart stencils in a few different sizes. Other valentine stencils—such as arrows and cupids—may also be created. Or the same stencil can be moved to different positions on a paper to create the Valentine's Day card.

Spatter Painting

1. Before creating the cards, students should practice making spatter-painted designs using a stencil. Place a heart stencil flat on a sheet of scrap paper.

2. Pour red tempera into a tray or dish. Dip an old toothbrush into the paint. Tap off any excess paint on the side of the tray or dish.

3. Hold the brush directly over the paper. Spatter color against the cutout heart and paper by moving a finger or a craft stick along the toothbrush bristles *toward* you (it is very important to move in this direction or the paint will splatter on the person moving the craft stick). Or spatter paint by rubbing the toothbrush over a piece of wire screen that is held directly over the paper.

4. Cover the paper with spatters. Children will need to experiment to make the spotted, small drops of splashes come out the way they want. If the toothbrush is too loaded with paint, for example, the spatters will become large blobs.

5. When the paint dries, remove the heart stencil. The stencil will leave behind a spatter-paint heart.

Making the Valentine's Day Cards

1. Arrange several valentine stencils (several hearts, or hearts and arrows and cupids) onto a sheet of drawing or construction paper. Place the stencils flat. Spatter-paint the card. Let the paint dry and remove the stencils.

2. Fold the paper in half with the stenciled spatter-painted design on the outside to make a card with a wraparound design. Write the valentine message inside.

3. Children will capture the hearts of their special valentines with these Stenciled Spatter-Painted Valentine's Day Cards!

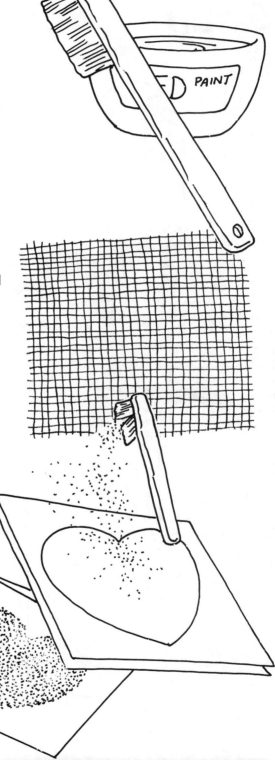

Ropes of Soap

What You Need

bits of soap

double boiler, stove or hot plate, and potholders
   for teacher

wooden stick or spoon

empty juice cans

newspaper (to work on)

heavy yarn of different colors, about 20 inches
   (50 cm) long for each can

nail file

What You Do

1. Lots of little pieces of leftover soap are often thrown away. Here's an idea for recycling those bits into special Valentine's Day gifts students can give family or friends.

2. Place all the bits of soap into the top of a double boiler. Put water into the bottom pan until it is about two-thirds full.

3. A teacher or other adult should do everything in step 3. Place the double boiler on a stove over a medium flame or on a hot plate. When the water begins to boil, lower the heat to a simmer and stir the soap with a wooden stick or spoon. Continue stirring until the pieces of soap have completely melted. Using potholders, lift off the top half of the double boiler. Pour the melted soap into empty juice cans placed on newspaper.

4. When the soap begins to cool, fold a 20-inch (50-cm) piece of heavy yarn in half. Put both ends of the yarn into the soap so that half the total yarn is inside the soap.

5. Allow the soap to harden thoroughly. Remove the soap from each can by dipping the can into warm water.

6. Working on newspaper, use a nail file to carve hearts into the sides of the soap. Carve out the initials or name of the person who will be receiving the Valentine gift. Ropes of Soap may also be designed with carvings of faces, figures, or abstract shapes.

Collage

Photograph, Letter, and Presidential Coin Rubbing Collages

A collage is a picture that uses a variety of materials, such as bits of magazines or newspapers, that are arranged and pasted onto a surface. It can consist of a combination of different materials or only one type.

What You Need

Photograph and Letter Collages

oaktag (or white cardboard) for surface

white glue

scissors

family photographs

magazines

newspapers

anything else you can think of for collage materials or for a different surface

Presidential Coin Rubbing Collage

Washington quarter

Lincoln penny

masking tape

thin paper (typing or computer paper)

crayons (with paper wrappings removed) or pencils of various colors

What You Do

1. When you design a collage, the most important thing is to use your imagination. The idea is to use ordinary objects—sometimes things we throw away—and arrange them so that they make an interesting picture. Collages are fun because they surprise people who look at them and recognize the different kinds of materials that are used in a creative way.

2. Assemble the materials you want to use. Think about using different shapes, textures, and colors. Place the materials on an oaktag sheet. Try several arrangements to see which one you like best. When you decide on one particular design, you're ready to glue. Simply lift each piece, dab a little glue on the back of it, and glue it in its place. Continue until you have glued all of the pieces onto the surface.

   Here are ideas for specific types of collages:

Photograph Collage

1. It's fun to make a collage of family photographs and mementos. Collect as many photos as you can. Then look for pictures of objects you associate with members

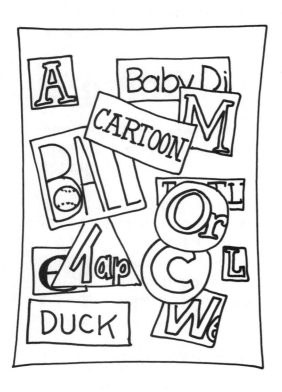

of your family. For example, if your sister collects baseball cards, you can include part of a card in your collage. Maybe your brother likes pretzels. Why not include part of the wrapping from a pretzel bag in your collage? You can include old greeting cards, postcards, movie ticket stubs, or even a piece from an old paper party hat—anything that makes you think of things your family likes or shares.

2. After gathering the photos and mementos, cut or tear them into interesting shapes. Then arrange them onto the background and glue them into place.

Letter Collage

Make a collage out of letters that you find in old magazines or newspapers. Cut out single letters or groups of letters that appeal to you. Arrange the letters onto a surface. You can position them in any way that pleases you—upside down, backward, or overlapping. Glue them, one at a time, onto the surface.

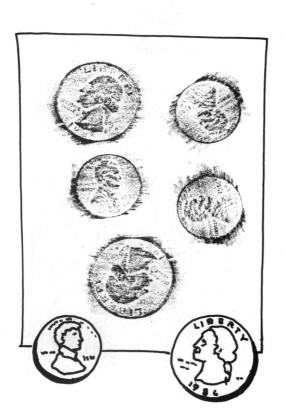

Presidential Coin Rubbing Collage

1. Celebrate George Washington's and Abraham Lincoln's birthdays by making rubbings of the coins that bear their pictures: a quarter for Washington and a penny for Lincoln. Then create a collage of the rubbings.

2. To make a coin rubbing, fold a small piece of masking tape over itself and stick it to the tail side of the coin so that you can temporarily attach it to a desk or tabletop. Place a sheet of typing or computer paper on top of the coin and rub with the side of an unwrapped crayon or pencils of various colors.

3. Hold the paper down firmly while rubbing, so that it doesn't slip and spoil the design. Make even strokes and move the crayon in the same direction. You're ''lifting'' the design from the surface. As you rub, you'll see Washington's or Lincoln's picture appear.

4. Make a collage of these presidential coin rubbings.

What You Need

bowl

needle

large raw eggs

water

teaspoon, vinegar, food coloring, teacup, spoon
(for dye)

paper towels (for drying eggs; to work on)

white glue

glitter (for Glitter-Initial Eggs)

uncooked rice or small beads, assorted colors (for
Egg Rolls)

wax paper (or other sheet of paper), toothpicks
(for Egg Rolls)

strong nylon thread (for hanging eggs)

buttons

Decorative Suspended Eggs

**Etch-an-Egg, Glitter-Initial Eggs,
and Egg Rolls**

What You Do

Blowing Eggs

1. Tell children that a decorated hard-boiled egg can be enjoyed for a short time, but will spoil quickly. To keep a decorated egg much longer, they can blow an egg from its shell.

2. Work over a bowl. Using a needle, the teacher should help a student puncture a small hole at one end of a raw egg. Make a slightly larger hole at the other end.

3. The student should blow gently into the smaller hole so that the egg comes out of the hole at the other end. Rinse out the egg with water and set it aside to dry. *Safety Note:* To avoid ingesting raw egg, children should *not* put their mouths against an egg when blowing into it.

Dyeing the Eggs

1. Dye eggs for the Etch-an-Egg and Glitter-Initial Eggs projects. Follow this recipe for making the dye: To 3/4 cup (180 ml) boiling water, add 2 teaspoons (10 ml) vinegar and food coloring for the desired shade. (About 15 drops works well for the Glitter-Initial Eggs. Make a bright, deep color for the etched eggs.) Stir. *Safety Note:* After the

teacher or other adult boils the water and pours it into a teacup, closely supervise as the students add the vinegar and food coloring.

2. Dip the egg into the cup of dye. When it's the desired shade, remove the egg from the dye with a spoon. Place the dyed egg on a paper towel to dry.

Etch-an-Egg

1. Tell students that etching is a method of engraving a design. The lines of the design are scratched with a needle on a surface that's coated with wax, dye, or a similar substance.

2. The children can get the feel of etching by using the point of a needle to scratch designs into a dyed egg. Use an egg that has been dyed a bright, deep color. Students should be careful not to puncture or crush the eggs as they scratch with the needles. Suggest etchings of spring chicks, spring flowers, or similar seasonal subject matter. Or they might like to Etch-an-Egg with an abstract design.

Glitter-Initial Eggs

1. Using a dyed egg, "write" a person's initial(s) with glue. Make the initial(s) large. Sprinkle one or more colors of glitter over the initial(s). Choose color(s) of glitter that contrast with the color of the background dye, so that the initial(s) stands out.

2. If desired, make the initial of the person's first name on one side of the egg. Allow the glue and glitter to dry. Then make the initial of the person's last name on the other side of the egg.

3. Create other types of Glitter Eggs. Use glue and glitter to make curls and swirls of color around the egg. Or paint a picture using glue and glitter.

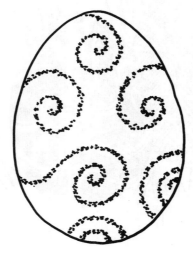

Egg Rolls

1. Eggs may be decorated with dyed rice or small beads of different colors. If using rice, refer to directions for coloring rice on page 49.

2. Put the rice or beads onto a sheet of wax paper (or other paper). Spread them out so there's a good mixture of color.

3. Spread glue on an area of the egg and gently ''roll'' the egg in the rice or beads. Use a toothpick to move away any rice (beads) that are blocking the holes at either end. Let the glue dry. Glue and roll the remaining parts in the same way until the whole egg (except for the holes) is covered with rice or beads.

4. Create other Egg Rolls using small, lightweight, colorful objects.

Suspending the Eggs

To display the decorated egg, suspend it vertically or horizontally. First, enlarge the holes at the ends of the egg slightly so that they're about 1/4 inch (1/2 cm) big. Then cut a 3-inch (7 1/2-cm) length of thread, insert it through a needle, and double it over.

1. For Horizontal Hanging:
Insert the double-threaded needle through the hole at the top and jiggle the needle around a little until it comes through the bottom hole. Adjust the thread so that an equal amount extends out of both ends of the egg. Cut off the needle and tie the two ends of thread together to form a hanger for the egg.

2. For Vertical Hanging:
Insert a double-threaded needle through a button hole (button should be slightly larger than hole in egg). Loop thread through the button several times and knot so that the button is fastened at the end of the thread. Insert the threaded needle through the bottom hole of the egg and jiggle upside down until the needle comes through the other hole. Turn the egg right-side-up so that the button will rest over the bottom hole. Cut off the needle, leaving the length of thread. Tie the thread near the top to make a hanging loop.

Two-Stick Kite

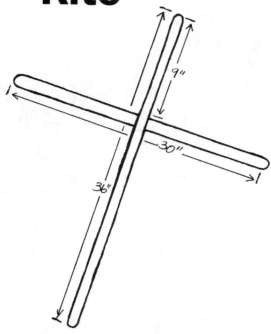

What You Need

crayons

ruler

wooden stick, 36 inches (90 cm) long, 1/4 inch (1/2 cm) or 1/2 inch (1 cm) wide (the upright stick)

wooden stick, 30 inches (75 cm) long, 1/4 inch (1/2 cm) or 1/2 inch (1 cm) wide (the cross stick)

white glue

strong cotton string (a full ball)

metal file (or small saw)

scissors

1 square yard (90 square cm) of gift wrap or butcher's paper (to cover kite)

several sheets of tissue paper

30 feet (9 m) of sewing thread

2 reinforcements

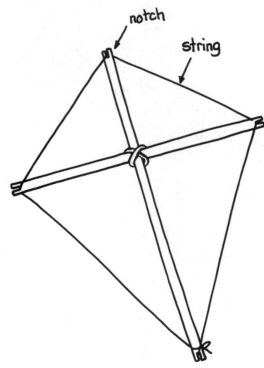

What You Do

1. Kites have been popular ever since their origin in China over 2,500 years ago. There are many different types of kites children can make. Try building this two-stick kite.

2. To make the frame, make a crayon mark 9 inches (23 cm) down from the top of the 36-inch (90-cm) upright stick. Make a crayon mark at the center of the 30-inch (75-cm) cross stick. Place the cross stick on top of the upright stick so that the crayon marks meet and the sticks form a cross. Glue the sticks together and secure them with string.

3. Use a metal file or small saw to make notches 1/4 inch (1/2 cm) deep in the ends of each stick. Run string around from end to end, inserting the string in each notch to form the diamond shape of the kite. Tie the string.

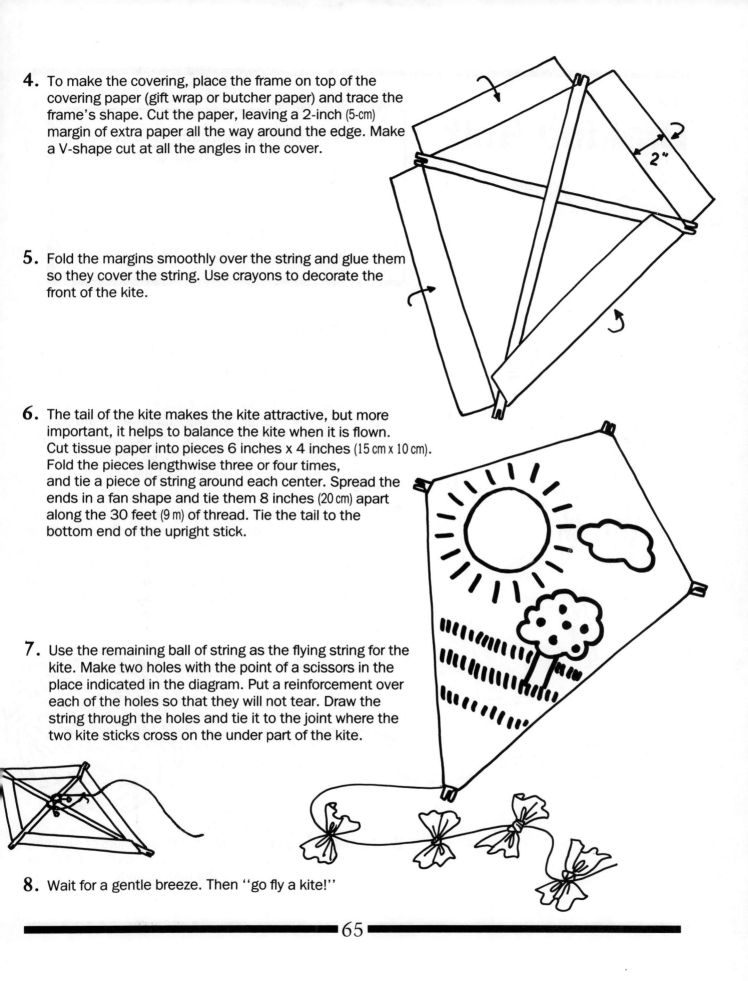

4. To make the covering, place the frame on top of the covering paper (gift wrap or butcher paper) and trace the frame's shape. Cut the paper, leaving a 2-inch (5-cm) margin of extra paper all the way around the edge. Make a V-shape cut at all the angles in the cover.

2"

5. Fold the margins smoothly over the string and glue them so they cover the string. Use crayons to decorate the front of the kite.

6. The tail of the kite makes the kite attractive, but more important, it helps to balance the kite when it is flown. Cut tissue paper into pieces 6 inches x 4 inches (15 cm x 10 cm). Fold the pieces lengthwise three or four times, and tie a piece of string around each center. Spread the ends in a fan shape and tie them 8 inches (20 cm) apart along the 30 feet (9 m) of thread. Tie the tail to the bottom end of the upright stick.

7. Use the remaining ball of string as the flying string for the kite. Make two holes with the point of a scissors in the place indicated in the diagram. Put a reinforcement over each of the holes so that they will not tear. Draw the string through the holes and tie it to the joint where the two kite sticks cross on the under part of the kite.

8. Wait for a gentle breeze. Then ''go fly a kite!''

Braided Belt

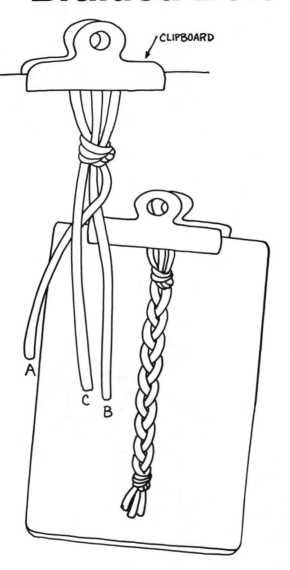

CLIPBOARD

A

C

B

What You Need

3 strands of string, 6 inches (15 cm) each, for practice

clipboard (or other method of holding string or yarn while working)

rug yarn: 3 strands of color A
          3 strands of color B
          3 strands of color C
          (3 colors of child's choice)

Each rug yarn strand should be 6 feet (1 3/4 m) long.

What You Do

1. Braid crafting can be used to make such items as belts, hats, and rugs. Try a braided belt. If students know how to braid, this will be an easy project for them. However, there are a few things to point out so that they will have attractive belts. When braiding, always work the outer strands *over* the center strand. They should keep the strands taut and out toward them, so that they have an even braid. They shouldn't twist the strands as they work.

2. Try a practice braid using three strands of string. Knot the three strands together near the top. Place the fringe above the knot under a clipboard. Begin on the right with strand A and move it *over* the middle strand, B. Take the strand on the left, C, and move it *over* what has become the middle strand, A. Continue alternating right and left strands *over* the middle strand. The finished practice piece should look as shown.

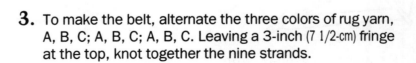

3. To make the belt, alternate the three colors of rug yarn, A, B, C; A, B, C; A, B, C. Leaving a 3-inch (7 1/2-cm) fringe at the top, knot together the nine strands.

4. Place the fringe under a clipboard. Work the first braid with the first three strands on the right-hand side. Begin with the right strand and move it over the center, then move the left strand over the center and so on. Work the braid flat and evenly until there are about 3 inches (7 1/2 cm) of yarn left at the bottom.

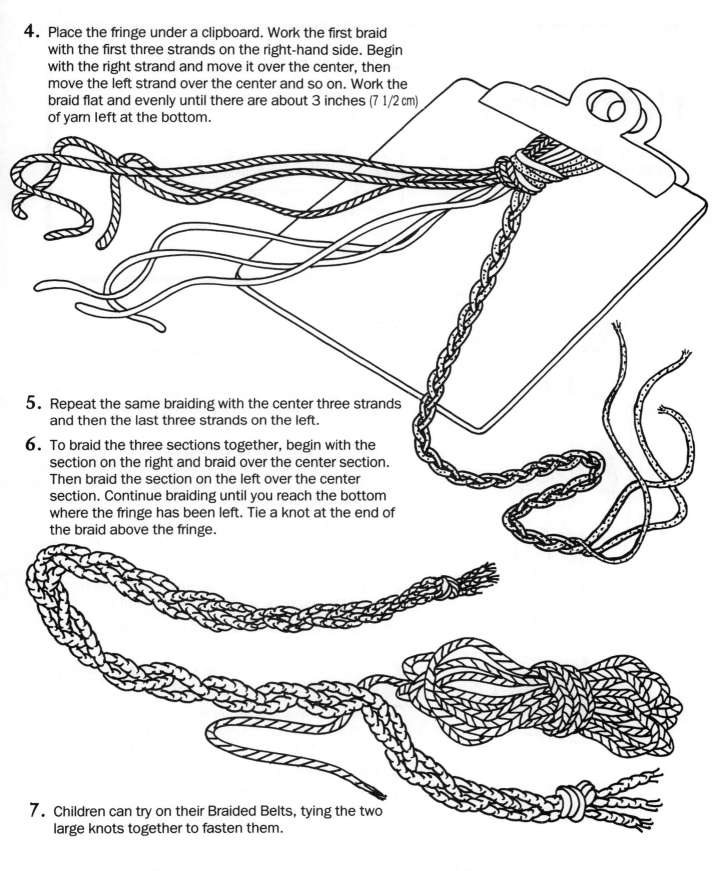

5. Repeat the same braiding with the center three strands and then the last three strands on the left.

6. To braid the three sections together, begin with the section on the right and braid over the center section. Then braid the section on the left over the center section. Continue braiding until you reach the bottom where the fringe has been left. Tie a knot at the end of the braid above the fringe.

7. Children can try on their Braided Belts, tying the two large knots together to fasten them.

Nutty Pins

Here are some "nutty" ideas for you to try.

What You Do

1. Draw the outline of an animal's shape on a piece of felt and cut it out.

2. Brush glue around the rim of a walnut shell half. Position the shell on the animal shape and press it down firmly until it sticks on the felt. Let it dry.

3. Add small pieces of different colors of felt for facial features and body parts. You can use markers of various colors on the nut or felt to highlight, outline, or decorate different parts of the animal.

4. Turn the animal shape over and insert a safety pin through the felt in the middle of the shape. Your nutty pin is ready to be worn.

5. Make as many nutty pins as you'd like for yourself or for your friends. Wear them to a "nutty pin party."

Another Nutty Idea: Make a nutty pin wall hanging as a decoration for your room.

1. Cut a strip of felt measuring about 2 inches wide (5 cm) and 2 feet long (60 cm).

2. Punch a hole in the center of the felt about 1/2 inch (1 cm) from the top. Pull yarn through the hole, tie the ends together, and hang the yarn from a nail or hook.

3. Pin your nutty pins to the felt strip. Keep adding pins as you create them. Remove a pin when you want to wear it. Try to come up with other "nutty" ideas.

What You Need

large wooden spool
4 small-headed thin nails
hammer
ball of yarn
bobby pin (opened)
scissors
needle and thread

Spool Weaving: "Plant Sitter" Mat

This is a quick and easy form of weaving. Using a spool as a loom, weave your way to a "plant sitter" mat.

What You Do

1. To prepare the spool, hammer 4 nails around the hole into the top of the spool. Try to position them evenly so that they form a square. Push the end of the yarn down through the hole in the spool. Allow about 3 inches (7 1/2 cm) of yarn to hang out below the spool. Prepare your loom by looping the yarn around each of the nails, as shown.

2. To weave, pass the yarn a second time around the outside of the first nail. Using a bobby pin, pull the bottom loop up and over the top loop. Lift it over the nail head and drop it down on the inside of the nail. Pass the yarn around the outside of the second nail and work in the same way. Continue weaving around the spool, always going around in the same direction. A woven rope will grow out of the bottom of the spool.

3. When the rope is 2 yards (1 3/4 m) long, cut off the yarn, leaving about 1 foot (30 cm) of unwoven yarn at the top. Weave the next nail. Then place the bobby pin beneath the loop that's left on the nail. Still working from the outside in, pull the loop until the loose end of yarn comes through. Repeat this process for each of the other three nails. Pull the loose end tight. Then cut it off next to the woven rope. Pull the rope down, removing it from the spool.

4. Wind the rope into a very tight circle, enlarging it until you have a round mat. Sew the circle together so that it does not separate. (You need to tack it only from the bottom.) "Sit" a pretty plant on top of the mat!

5. You can try making other articles by weaving ropes and sewing them together in strips or circles.

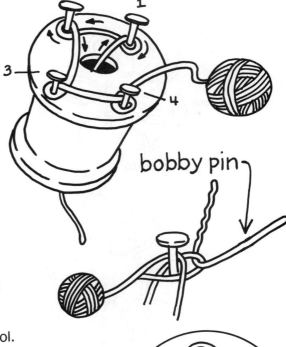

bobby pin

APRIL
Wire Flowers

What You Do

1. Ask students if they've ever wired (sent) flowers to anyone. Tell them this is another way to "wire" flowers. They can use their fingers to shape wire into flowers. Here are some suggestions.

2. Wind the wire around the index finger several times to get started. Remove the wire from the finger and keep turning the circle around and around so that it increases in size as more wire is added. When the circular part of the flower is the desired size, continue adding wire, moving out from the spiral and back in again to make petals. Repeat this in-and-out shaping until you return to the first petal.

3. Leaving a small piece of extra wire, cut the wire flower off from the spool. Twist the extra piece of wire around a petal on the flower. Put the flower aside.

4. Try another flower, following this suggestion. Make small loops, one after the other, forming them into a circular shape for the center of the flower. To form a loop, make the wire cross itself.

5. Repeat this looping, moving around and around from the center of the flower out, until the flower is the desired size. End it by cutting the wire from the spool and twisting the extra piece around another part of the flower.

6. Students can design other flowers of their own, making a bouquet of about five flowers.

7. To add the stems, cut a piece of wire twice the desired length of the stem for the flower. Bend the wire in half and twist the ends together, so that the stem is sturdy (double thickness). Attach the stem to the bottom part of one of the flowers by twisting the end of the stem wire around the wire on the flower. Add stems to each of the flowers, varying the lengths slightly so that the flowers will be different heights.

8. Choose a container large enough to provide a stable base for the flowers. Then decorate the container. (Some ideas: glue on scraps of fabric, tissue paper, and so on. Or use adhesive-backed paper.)

9. Make a small hole in the lid of the container. Place one of the wire stems through the hole. Decide on an arrangement for the flowers. Then make holes for each of the other flowers and add them to the container. Try bending several of the stems in different directions. Display the bouquet of Wire Flowers.

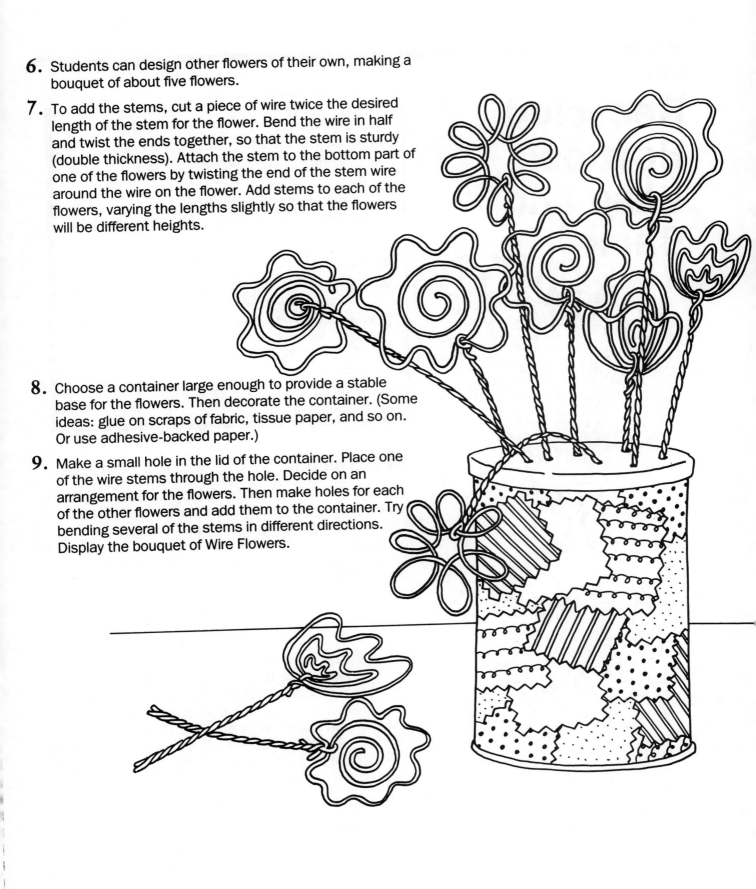

Recycled Bottles: Vase and Bank

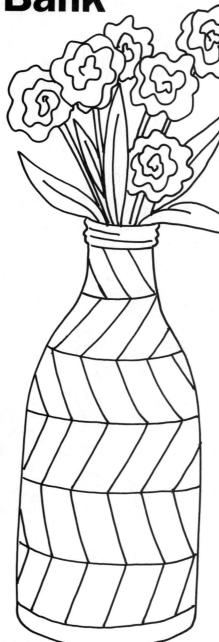

What You Need

Vase

quart-size (liter) bottle (any shape)

adhesive tape, 1/2 inch (1 cm) width

scissors

acrylic paints and paintbrushes

acrylic gloss medium and varnish and brush
(optional) *for teacher*

Bank

bottle (any shape with neck large enough for coins
to fit through) with lid

3 colors of yarn (directions for measuring amount
needed for the bottle selected are given in step
1 of bank project)

paper clips

clipboard

white glue

What You Do

Children can help the environment by recycling bottles. They can use empty bottles for vases, banks, candleholders, or purely as decorative objects. For starters, they can try the following two ways of decorating empty bottles. Prepare the bottles by cleaning the insides and outsides. If necessary, soak the bottles in hot water to remove the labels. Dry the bottles thoroughly.

Vase

1. Cut the adhesive tape into 2-inch (5-cm) strips. Beginning at the neck of the bottle and working down to the bottom, adhere tape on a diagonal, putting one row of tape at an angle from left to right, and the next row of tape at an angle from right to left. This will create a crisscross pattern. Continue in this way until the entire surface of the bottle is covered from top to bottom. Add small pieces of tape to fill in any holes.

2. Use acrylic paint to color the taped bottle.

3. When the paint is dry, the teacher or another adult can add a coat of acrylic gloss medium and varnish for protection and to give the vase an extra shine.

Bank

1. To figure out how much yarn will be needed to cover the bottle, take one of the three colors of yarn and wind it around the bottle in a single layer, starting at the neck and working your way down. Make sure the entire surface is covered. Mark the place on the yarn with a paper clip and unwrap the bottle. Double the length to have enough to make a braid and cut the yarn. Use the first piece of yarn to measure the other two colors.

2. Tie a knot at the top of the three pieces of colorful yarn to join them. Braid the three pieces together. Use a clipboard to help keep the yarn taut and even while braiding. Braid almost to the bottom and tie a knot at the end to secure the braid. (If necessary, refer children to pages 66–67 for instructions on braiding.)

3. Begin at the neck of the bottle and wind the braid tightly around the bottle, glueing as the braid is wrapped. The easiest way is to put a small amount of glue around about 1 inch (2 1/2 cm) of the bottle and firmly stick the braid onto the glued surface. Continue glueing and wrapping until the entire bank is covered with the braid. Make a slit in the lid and place on bottle.

4. Encourage students to recycle bottles rather than discard them.

APRIL
Mirrored Mosaic

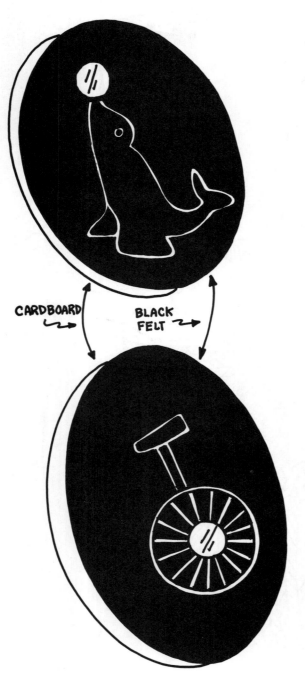

CARDBOARD

BLACK FELT

What You Need

sheet of cardboard
scissors
piece of black felt (same size as cardboard)
white glue
small pocket mirror (any shape)
pencil or chalk
other small pieces of felt (assorted colors)
ruler

What You Do

1. Explain to students that they can make a mosaic frame for a mirror by arranging cut pieces of felt and a small pocket mirror on cardboard so that everything forms a picture.

2. Cut the cardboard into a large oval shape. (Save the leftover pieces for a mirror stand.) Cut the black felt into an oval shape the same size as the cardboard oval. Glue the black felt onto the cardboard.

3. Decide what kind of picture to make, thinking about how the mirror can be part of the design. Keep it simple. For example, a circular mirror might be used as a ball that a seal balances, a wheel on a unicycle or car, or the door of a house. Draw the picture on the felt, tracing around the mirror.

4. Spread some glue on the back of the mirror and press it down in position on the felt-covered cardboard.

5. To make the mosaic, cut out a small piece of one color of felt, dab a little glue on the back, and press it onto the black felt so that it fits within the picture.

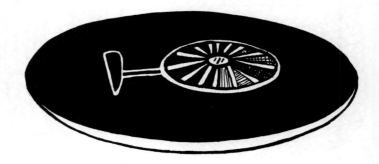

6. Cut out a piece of another color of felt, glue the back, and press it down near the first piece, leaving a little space between. By leaving a small space around each piece of the different colors of felt, the black background shows through. This will outline each shape and create the mosaic effect.

7. Keep cutting assorted colors of felt shapes, glueing them down and leaving space for the black outline, until the picture is filled in with the mosaic design.

8. Make a mirror stand. Cut a piece of the leftover cardboard into a strip 3 1/2 inches (9 cm) wide and a little longer than half the height of the oval. Bend as shown and glue it to the back of the oval-shaped cardboard.

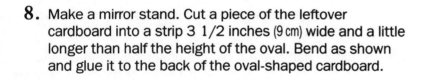

3½"

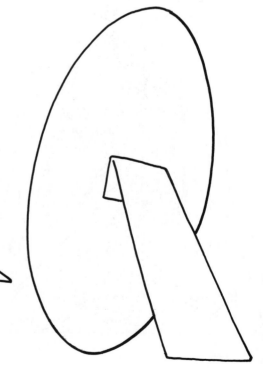

9. The Mirrored Mosaic is ready for viewing. ''Here's looking at you!''

Embossing: Framed-Foil Flyers

What You Need

newspaper
shoe-box lid
clear tape
aluminum foil
ballpoint pens

TAPE

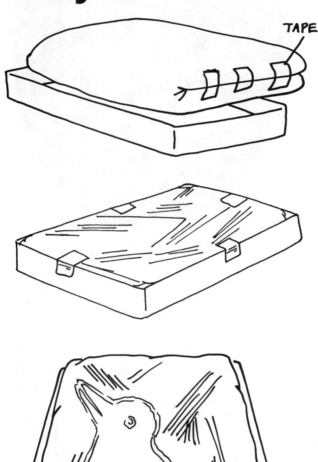

What You Do

1. Tell students they can *emboss* a picture in aluminum foil. *Embossing* means that as students decorate the foil with a tool, they will press down into the foil. When the foil is turned over, the designs will then be raised up from the flat surface.

2. Begin by framing the foil. Fit a pad of folded newspaper into a shoe-box lid and tape the paper's edges together to keep them from unfolding.

3. Lift the newspaper pad out of the lid and wrap a piece of aluminum foil around it, carefully smoothing the foil down on the paper. Tape the foil onto the taped side of the paper.

4. Put the foil-covered newspaper back into the lid, with the taped part underneath. Attach the foil to the lid with a few small pieces of tape. This creates a frame for the foil picture.

5. Students can make a picture of something that flies, such as an airplane, a kite, a bird, a butterfly, or another insect. Using a ballpoint pen as the embossing tool, draw the outline of the flyer-shape on the foil. Make it big enough to cover a large area of the foil.

6. Fill in the details, working slowly and carefully. Make certain that the foil rests flat on the pad of newspapers so that the pen doesn't tear through the foil. Lightly press different types of lines, dots, curves, and swirls into the surface of the foil. Work small areas at a time. When finished, remove tape and turn foil over so that raised design shows. Retape around newspaper and frame before displaying the Framed-Foil Flyers.

7. Create other Framed-Foil pictures.

What You Need

2 sheets of cardboard
compass
scissors
yarn sewing needle
10 yards (9 m) of yarn
1 piece of felt (to cover one piece of cardboard)
white glue
felt scraps

3-D Pompon Pictures

Now that spring is officially here, you can greet it with spring flowers. Pompons make a picture three-dimensional—so you want to reach out and touch it.

What You Do

1. To make a pompon, from one sheet of cardboard cut two circles, each 2 inches (5 cm) in diameter. Cut a center hole about 1/2 inch (1 cm) in diameter in each of the circles.

2. Thread the needle with a 4-yard (3 1/2-m) length of yarn. Double it over so that it becomes 2 yards (1 3/4 m) long. Hold both circles together. Leaving a small tail of yarn as an anchor, pass the needle through the center hole, over the outside edge, and through the center again. Keep winding the yarn evenly over the cardboard circles until the center hole is filled in.

3. Holding the center of the circles and turning as you go along, use scissors to cut through the yarn between the outer edges of the two circles.

CARDBOARD CIRCLES

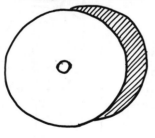

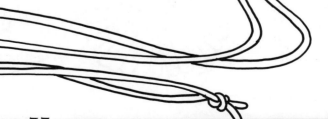

77

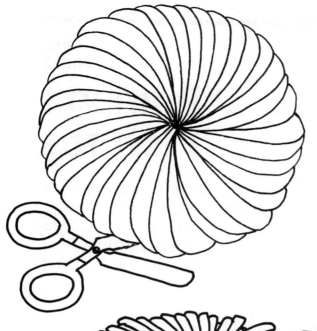

4. Double a 24-inch (60-cm) strand of yarn in half. Slip the doubled-up yarn between the cardboard circles. Pull the yarn up tightly and tie it very firmly around the center of the yarn circle. Remove the cardboard and fluff out the pompon by rolling it between your hands. Leave the two ends of the tying yarn for use later. Make a second pompon in the same way.

5. To make the picture, cover the second sheet of cardboard by glueing the large piece of felt on top of it. This will be the background for your picture. Decide where you would like the flowers to be in the picture.

6. To attach each pompon, use scissors to poke two little holes through the felt-covered cardboard. Pull the two ends of the tying yarn through the holes and knot them together in back of the cardboard.

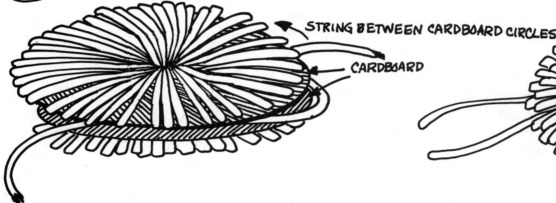

STRING BETWEEN CARDBOARD CIRCLES

CARDBOARD

7. Use the felt scraps to create the rest of your picture. You might make stems and leaves for your flowers and place them in a vase or in a garden with trees.

CARDBOARD   FELT

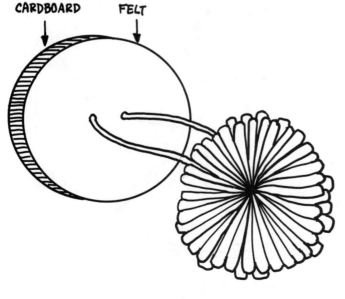

Potpourri

What You Need

fragrant flower petals

herb leaves (mint, bay, thyme)

newspaper (for drying petals and leaves)

large jar and cover

spices (whole allspice, whole cloves, cinnamon sticks)

salt

large spoon

small jars or small net bags (or netting)

colorful ribbons

What You Do

1. Students can make a sweet-smelling surprise for Mom this Mother's Day—a jar or sachet of potpourri.

2. Gather petals of flowers that smell good. There are many combinations that may be used, depending on availability. Students can experiment with petals from different types of flowers. Rose petals and rosebuds are great. Other flowers that work well include lilac, violet, orange blossom, jasmine, magnolia, carnation, and honeysuckle. Herb leaves, such as mint, bay, and thyme, may also be used.

3. Spread the flower petals and herb leaves out on sheets of newspaper in a well-ventilated area to dry. They should be turned every few days so that the air dries all sides. Keep them out of direct sunlight. Drying time takes one to two weeks.

4. When the petals and leaves are dry, put them in a big jar. Mix them together with broken-up cinnamon sticks, whole cloves, and whole allspice. Sprinkle the mixture with a little salt. (Salt helps absorb moisture.) Stir the mixture every few days. Leave the potpourri in the covered jar for about a week.

5. Package the potpourri. Make a sachet by putting the potpourri in a net bag (or netting) and tying it with a pretty ribbon. Or put the potpourri in a small jar or basket and tie a decorative ribbon around it. You may wish to cover a basket with plastic wrap to transport it.

Sponge Marionette

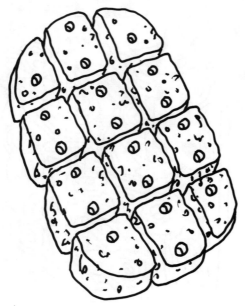

What You Need

oval-shaped dry sponges (2 for each marionette)
scissors
thin steel wire
wire cutters
fine-line markers (optional)
wooden craft sticks (6 for each marionette)
masking tape
rubber band
string—three pieces 17 inches (42 cm) long, one
  piece 13 inches (32 cm) long, one piece
  26 inches (65 cm) long

What You Do

1. Children can use dry sponges to create marionettes—puppets with jointed bodies that are moved by strings. Make the body parts. Cut one sponge into two pieces for the head and body. Cut the other sponge into twelve pieces for the arms and legs. Make holes in each of the sponge pieces in the places shown in the diagram.

2. Put thin steel wire through the holes to connect the parts, shaping each wire piece into a ring and twisting the ends together. The wire rings serve as the joints that allow the parts to move freely. Facial features and other decorations can be added using fine-line markers.

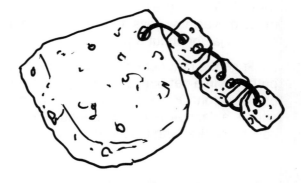

3. Prepare the control sticks. Wooden craft sticks with string attached can be used to control the marionette. Tape two sticks together to make one long stick. Tape two more sticks together. Cross the sticks in the middle and secure them with a rubber band. Tape together two more sticks, but do not attach them to the crossed sticks.

4. To attach the string, follow the diagram.
THE HEAD: Put one 17-inch (42-cm) string through the ring above the head. Tape each end onto stick A.
THE BODY: Put the 13-inch (32-cm) string through the middle hole in the sponge body and knot it. Tape the other end onto stick B.
THE ARMS: Tie the ends of the 26-inch (65-cm) string onto the wire rings at the wrists. Tape the center of the string onto stick B.
THE LEGS: Tie the two remaining 17-inch (42-cm) strings to the wire rings at the knees. Tape the other ends onto stick C.

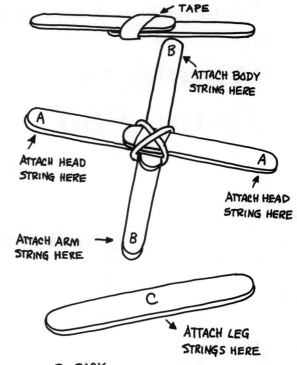

5. Students can control the marionette by moving the wooden sticks or by holding the controls in one hand and moving the strings with the other hand. The crossed sticks, A and B, control the head, body, and arms. The unattached stick, C, controls the legs.

6. Make the marionette walk by moving the leg control stick forward and tipping each side. Lift the string attached to the back of the marionette to make it lean over and bow. Students can practice making their marionettes wave, sit, jump, and dance. They might like to put on a Sponge Marionette puppet show.

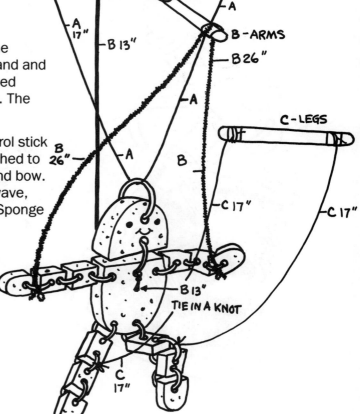

Marbleized Memo Pad

What You Need

large flat pan

boiling water *for teacher*

crayon shavings of different colors

drinking straw

2 sheets of white shelf paper (cut same size as typewriter paper)

pencil

2 sheets of cardboard

scissors

20 sheets of typewriter or computer paper

white glue

hole punch

3 pieces of thin leather strips, colorful yarn, or cord—about 1 foot (30 cm) long

What You Do

1. Here's a "marbleous" way to keep memos together.

2. *Safety Note:* A teacher or another adult should fill a large pan with boiling water. Teacher should closely supervise students at all times during the marbleizing part (steps 3 and 4) of the project, because of the boiling water.

3. Children can add crayon shavings of different colors to the water. Let the shavings melt. Blow gently with a straw to separate any large lumps of color.

4. Place a piece of shelf paper on the surface, draw it over the water, and lift it up. The spots of melted crayons will stick to the paper and form a marbleized pattern. Using the same process, make a marblelike design on the other piece of shelf paper.

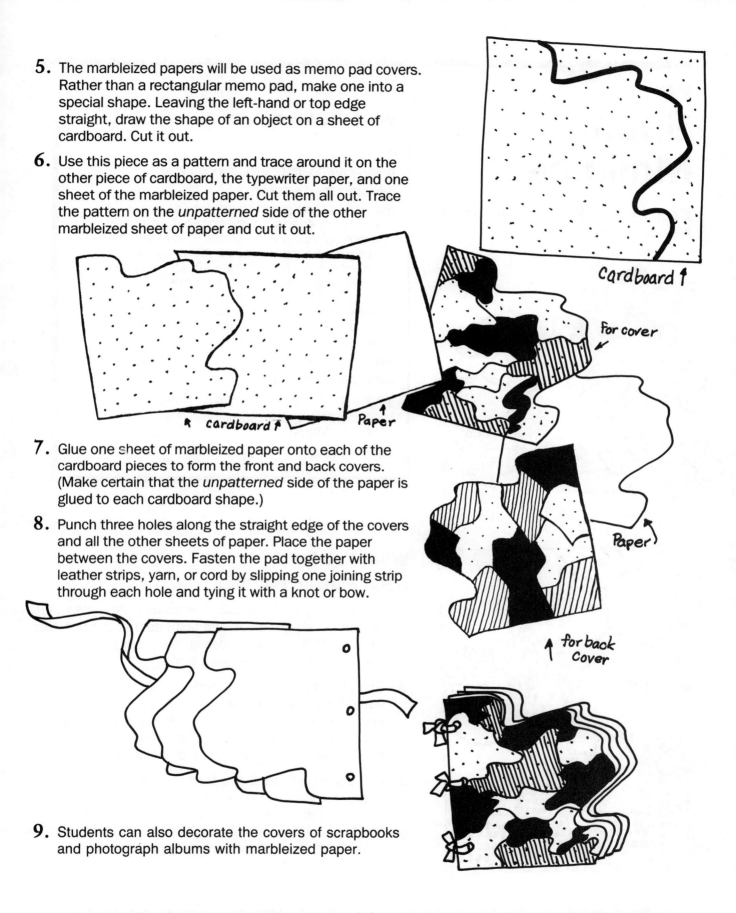

5. The marbleized papers will be used as memo pad covers. Rather than a rectangular memo pad, make one into a special shape. Leaving the left-hand or top edge straight, draw the shape of an object on a sheet of cardboard. Cut it out.

6. Use this piece as a pattern and trace around it on the other piece of cardboard, the typewriter paper, and one sheet of the marbleized paper. Cut them all out. Trace the pattern on the *unpatterned* side of the other marbleized sheet of paper and cut it out.

Cardboard

cardboard

Paper

for cover

Paper

for back Cover

7. Glue one sheet of marbleized paper onto each of the cardboard pieces to form the front and back covers. (Make certain that the *unpatterned* side of the paper is glued to each cardboard shape.)

8. Punch three holes along the straight edge of the covers and all the other sheets of paper. Place the paper between the covers. Fasten the pad together with leather strips, yarn, or cord by slipping one joining strip through each hole and tying it with a knot or bow.

9. Students can also decorate the covers of scrapbooks and photograph albums with marbleized paper.

Seed Mosaics

Seed Mosaic Pictures and Seed Mosaic Maps

What You Need

pencil

heavy cardboard or thin, sanded wood

newspaper (to work on)

assorted seeds (such as sesame seeds;
sunflower seeds; seeds from butternut and
acorn squash; poppy seeds; cucumber seeds;
pumpkin seeds; birdseed; citrus fruit seeds
[orange, lemon, and grapefruit]; melon seeds
[cantaloupe, honeydew, watermelon]; rice;
white and black whole peppercorns; popcorn
kernels; red, white, yellow corn kernels; dried
yellow or green peas; dried beans [lima beans,
coffee beans]; and so on)

white glue and paintbrushes

tweezers (optional)

clear plastic wrap and transparent tape (optional)

food coloring, spoon, small bowl (for Seed
Mosaic Maps)

paper towels

What You Do
Seed Mosaic Pictures

1. Seeds are great for mosaics because of the wide variety
   of shapes, sizes, colors, and textures that can be used.
   Draw a simple picture or design on a sheet of heavy
   cardboard or on thin, sanded wood.

2. Spread out newspaper to work on. Students should have
   a handful of each kind of seed they'd like to use. They
   should decide what kinds of seeds would work best in
   each part of the picture (the sizes, shapes, textures, and
   colors—or contrasts of light and dark seeds).

3. Use one type of seed at a time. "Paint" glue on all parts
   of the picture that will be covered with that type of seed.
   Fill in the parts by sprinkling on small seeds. Add large
   seeds separately, placing each down individually by hand
   or with tweezers. Allow the glue to dry thoroughly.

4. Continue in the same way with each part of the picture and the remaining types of seeds, until the entire design is covered with a variety of seeds. Let the mosaic dry flat overnight.

5. If desired, cover the Seed Mosaic Picture with plastic wrap and tape the back.

Seed Mosaic Maps

1. Students can try their hand at mapmaking using the seed mosaic technique. They can work together in small groups.

2. Draw the outline and details of the map on thick cardboard or on thin, sanded wood. Spread glue along the outline and add seeds. For example, if making a map of the United States, try black watermelon seeds or whole black peppercorns to outline the borders of each state and the borders of the country.

3. Fill in the outlines by spreading glue and adding seeds in the same way as for the Seed Mosaic Pictures. The natural colors of the seeds will lend a variety of colors to the map. Students might use dried green peas to show forest areas or national parks. If certain other colors are needed, use dyed rice.

4. For example, to create bodies of water on the map, dye white rice with blue food coloring and water. (See Rice Painting project on page 49 for instructions on coloring rice.) Spread dyed rice on paper towels and allow it to dry thoroughly before adding it to the mosaic. Different shades of blue rice can be sprinkled on for lakes and rivers. If covering a large area, such as an ocean, spread blue-colored rice with the back of a spoon.

5. Layers of large beans interspersed with smaller seeds can create a 3-D mountain range effect. (On a very large map or mural, lima beans can be used at the top of a range for a "snow-capped" mountain.)

6. Students can make a map key at the bottom by glueing individual seeds (for example, green peas for a forest area) that correspond to features on the map.

7. Display and use the Seed Mosaic Maps when studying a specific geographic area.

Jewelry at a Clip

With a little imagination, paper clips can be turned into unusual jewelry!

What You Need

1 box paper clips
scissors
ruler
1/4 yard (22 cm) colorful or predecorated adhesive-backed paper

adhesive backed paper

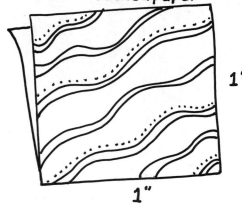

1"

1"

What You Do

1. To make a chain, link together two paper clips.

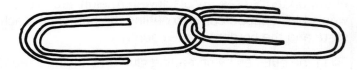

2. Continue joining clips, one after another, until you have a chain of twenty. Place the chain aside for the time being.

3. Here's how to cover the chain. Cut 20 squares, 1 inch x 1 inch (2 1/2 cm x 2 1/2 cm), from the adhesive-backed paper.

4. Peel off the backing from one square. Wrap the adhesive paper around the center of the first clip, pressing the paper down firmly and smoothly as you wrap.

5. Continue peeling and wrapping in this way, until you have covered all twenty clips.

6. Add a clip to one end of the chain and attach it to the clip at the other end. This serves as a clasp with which to open and close your jewelry.

7. Try on your neck clips.

8. You can add clip designs to the chain.

9. Make as many different designs as you'd like. Perhaps you'd like to create a clip belt by making a chain big enough to go around your waist. Or try linking neck clips or clip belts in double strands. Experiment and have fun with your Jewelry at a Clip.

What You Need

6 empty tin cans, with tops removed
   (assorted sizes)

large nail

hammer

cardboard roller (from paper towels, tin foil, or
   clear plastic wrap)

adhesive-backed paper or tin foil (to cover and
   decorate roller)

3 pieces of cord, each 36 inches (90 cm) long

1 piece of cord, 42 inches (105 cm) long

Note: Adult supervision required for this project.

Tin-Can Chimes

*Catch those spring breezes with
wind chimes made from tin cans.*

What You Do

1. Soak off or peel away any paper wrappings from the cans
you have selected. Clean the insides thoroughly with
soap and water and dry the cans.

2. Using a nail and a hammer, puncture a hole in the center
of each can's base.

3. To prepare the hanger, first decorate the cardboard roller
with adhesive-backed paper, or wrap it in tin foil.

4. Then tie each of the three 36-inch (90-cm) pieces of cord
around the roller so that they are evenly spaced and so
that they hang down. Tie each end of the 42-inch (105-cm)
cord around the roller near the ends. This cord is the
hanger.

5. String the six cans onto the three cords in an interesting
arrangement. Use a nail to help you push the cord down
into each can's hole. Knot the cord inside the can,
beneath the hole, to hold the can up. Plan your spacing
on each cord. Keep in mind that in order to chime, the
cans must knock into one another when the wind moves
them.

6. Hang your Tin-Can Chimes near a window or in another
place where a breeze will stir them. You'll soon be
"chiming in" with the tin-can sounds.

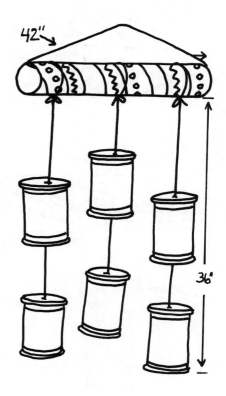

Sand-Cast Footprints

What You Need

newspaper (to work on)

shoe box (for foot cast)

sand (to fill shoe box)

water

disposable plastic container or large tin can (to hold water and the plaster mixture)

cornstarch

spoon

1 cup (250 ml) water, at room temperature

2 cups (500 ml) plaster of Paris

Safety Note: Read and follow warning on container. Plaster creates dust. Teacher should mix plaster outdoors or in a separate ventilated area. Do not cast any body parts because it can result in serious burns.
In this project the foot is put into the sand, *not* the plaster.

What You Do

1. Explain to students that casting is a process that allows one to make a plaster copy of an object or a shape. A cast is formed in a mold by using a plaster substance and letting it harden. The copy has the form and detail of the original.

2. Discuss with students how summer is a time for walking on the beach and making footprints in the sand. Tell them that in this project they will make footprints in the sand—but that these prints will not be washed away by the ocean's waves.

3. Spread out some newspaper on the floor. Fill the shoe box with sand, leaving about 1/2 inch (1 cm) space at the top. Add some water to make the sand firm but not too wet. Press down the entire foot flat into the sand to make a footprint.

4. Completely cover the print and the area around it by sprinkling a thin layer of cornstarch over it. The powdery cornstarch keeps the sand from sticking to the plaster.

5. Put 1 cup (250 ml) room-temperature water into a container. A teacher or another adult should add 2 cups (500 ml) plaster of Paris to the water. Mix, stirring until the mixture is smooth and feels about as thick as melted ice cream. If the mixture is not thick enough, add a little more powder.

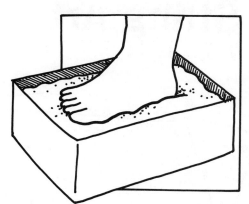

6. Using a spoon, children should carefully add the plaster of Paris to the footprint, filling in all areas of the print. Then spoon, or slowly pour, the rest of the plaster of Paris over the remaining sand. Add it evenly over the entire surface, using up all of the mixture.

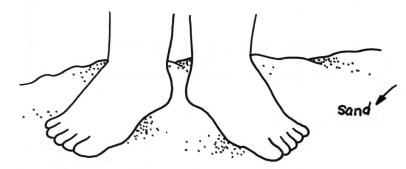

sand

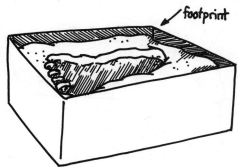

footprint

7. Wipe the spoon immediately and put aside the empty container for recycling. *Never pour plaster of Paris down the sink drain because it will harden and clog the pipes.*

8. Let the plaster of Paris cast harden for one hour. Remove the cast from the shoe box. Turn the cast over to see a plaster cast of the foot.

9. There will probably be some sand around the footprint. Do not remove the sand yet. Place the cast on a sheet of newspaper and allow it to dry overnight or longer. When the Sand-Cast Footprint is completely dry, brush off some of the sand, or leave it on for a textured effect.

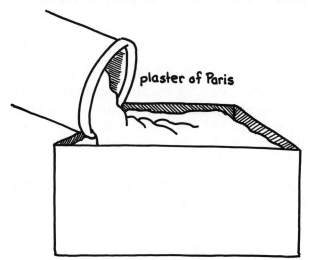

plaster of Paris

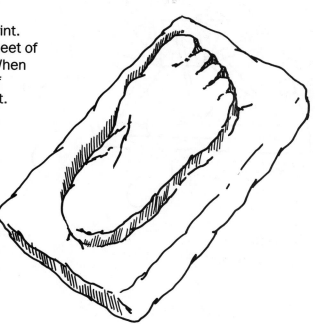

String Art

What You Need

newspaper (to work on)

sandpaper

piece of wood about 10 inches x 10 inches (25 cm x 25 cm) and 1/2 inch (1 cm) thick

acrylic paint and brushes (any color for background)

acrylic gloss medium and varnish and brush (*for teacher;* optional)

12 short nails

hammer

string (any color or thickness), at least 6 feet (2 m)

What You Do

1. Children can string their way into art. String Art pictures are fun to create and can be given as gifts for birthdays, holidays, and special occasions. Children can make one for Dad this Father's Day.

2. Spread out some newspaper to work on. Use sandpaper to smooth the edges of the wood. Brush off any wood dust. Paint the wood surface and edges with acrylic paint. Allow the paint to dry.

3. A teacher or another adult can cover the painted wood with a coat of acrylic gloss medium and varnish to protect the wood and to give it a shine. Let it dry.

4. To make the framework, arrange the nails in any desired pattern. Keep in mind that the string will be wound around the nails to create the picture, so try to position the nails at least 2 inches (5 cm) apart. Leaving room between the nail head and the wooden surface for string, hammer the nails into the wood.

5. Create the picture by winding the string around the nails. Children can, for example, "string" around a nail once, move on to another, and then come back to the same nail. Pull the string so that the line is straight from nail to nail. This will create a spider-web effect.

6. When the picture is finished, knot the string around the last nail and cut off the remaining string.

Potato-Printed Stationery

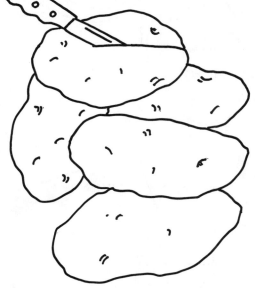

What You Need

small kitchen knife (not too sharp)
raw potatoes
towel (paper or cloth)
pencil
scrap paper
tempera and paintbrushes
small hand mirror (optional)
paper (any size desired for stationery)
white glue
clear tape

Note: Adult supervision required for this project.

What You Do

1. Children can carve potatoes into shapes that may be used to print repeating patterns on their own stationery.

2. Cut the potato in half. Dry the white flat surface with a towel so that the vegetable's juices won't interfere with the printing. Draw several simple summer designs on a piece of scrap paper, such as a beach ball, fish, sailboat, or seashell. Select one of the designs and paint it onto the surface of the potato. Let the paint dry.

3. Cut away all the parts of the potato surface *except* those where the design is painted to create a carved potato stamp.

4. Children may wish to carve their own initials to personalize the stationery. If they use initials, they should first write them on a piece of paper. Then hold a hand mirror in front of the initials. Paint the initials on the potato the way they look in the mirror and allow them to dry. Then carve out the initials as explained in step 3.

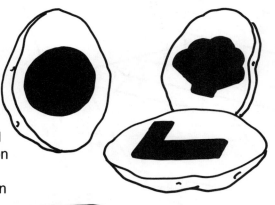

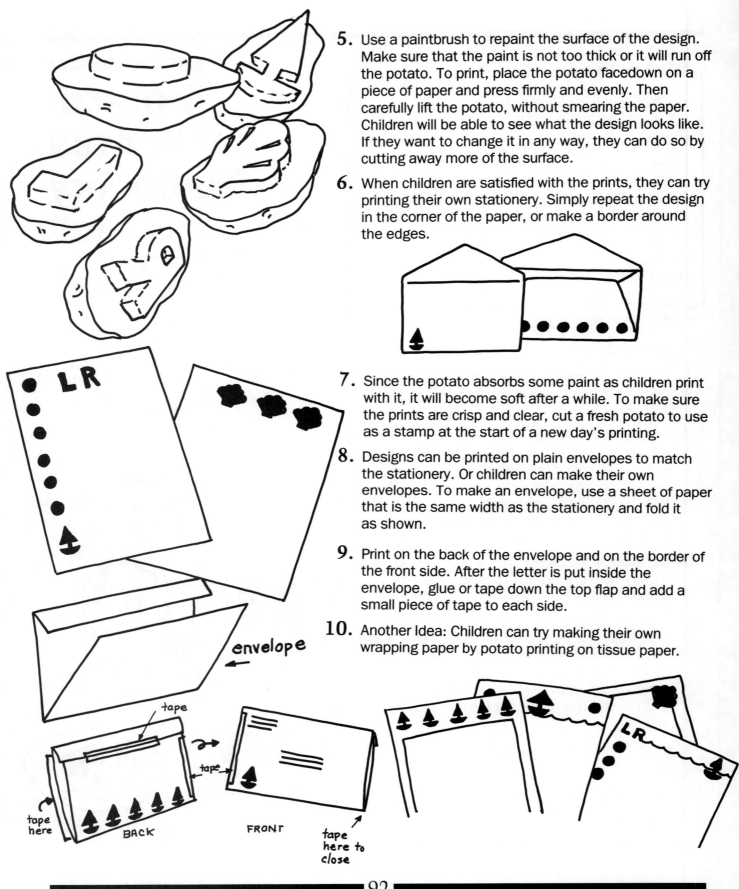

5. Use a paintbrush to repaint the surface of the design. Make sure that the paint is not too thick or it will run off the potato. To print, place the potato facedown on a piece of paper and press firmly and evenly. Then carefully lift the potato, without smearing the paper. Children will be able to see what the design looks like. If they want to change it in any way, they can do so by cutting away more of the surface.

6. When children are satisfied with the prints, they can try printing their own stationery. Simply repeat the design in the corner of the paper, or make a border around the edges.

7. Since the potato absorbs some paint as children print with it, it will become soft after a while. To make sure the prints are crisp and clear, cut a fresh potato to use as a stamp at the start of a new day's printing.

8. Designs can be printed on plain envelopes to match the stationery. Or children can make their own envelopes. To make an envelope, use a sheet of paper that is the same width as the stationery and fold it as shown.

9. Print on the back of the envelope and on the border of the front side. After the letter is put inside the envelope, glue or tape down the top flap and add a small piece of tape to each side.

10. Another Idea: Children can try making their own wrapping paper by potato printing on tissue paper.

envelope

tape

tape

tape here

BACK

FRONT

tape here to close

Seashell Stationery Holders and Seashell Notecards

What You Need

aluminum foil (to work on)

talc-free self-hardening clay

ruler

2 large scallop shells or 2 clamshells

assorted small shells

acrylic or tempera and paintbrushes

scissors

construction paper (or other heavyweight paper for seashell notecards)

white glue

fine-line markers

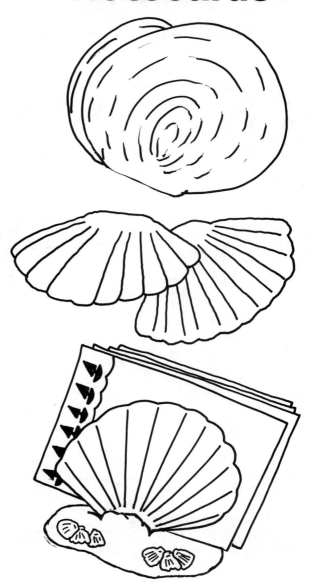

What You Do

1. Children can keep in touch with friends during the summer—whether away at camp, traveling, or at home—by writing letters. Seashell Stationery Holders are a great way to make paper and envelopes easily accessible.

2. Put a piece of tin foil on a flat surface. To make the holder base, shape two large handfuls of self-hardening clay into one big ball. Put the clay ball on the foil. Press it down, using the palm of the hand to form a flat circle about 3/4 inch (2 cm) thick and 5 inches (12 1/2 cm) in diameter. If the circle is not large enough, roll the clay into a ball again, add more clay, and repeat the process. Follow the directions for making either the Scallop or Clamshell holders.

Scallop Shell Stationery Holder

1. Center two large scallop shells on the clay base about 2 inches (5 cm) apart, standing with the insides facing each other. Press the shells into the clay so that the bottoms and ''tab'' parts of the shells are firmly wedged into the base. Gently press a little extra clay against the shells and base.

2. Add a cluster of small shells behind each of the scallop shells, creating an interesting arrangement. Insert them into the clay base so that they will remain securely in place when the clay dries. Do not decorate between the

scallop shells or along their sides. This area should be left unadorned so that the stationery may later rest on the base between the two shells.

3. Allow the clay to dry thoroughly. Drying time takes about a week.

4. If desired, paint the clay base, taking care not to get paint on the shells.

5. Insert some Potato-Printed Stationery (see pages 91–92), Seashell Notecards, or other stationery between the two scallop shells. Add enough stationery to fill the space between the two Seashell Stationery Holders.

Clamshell Stationery Holder

1. Capture the summer by painting summer scenes on the insides of two clamshells with acrylic paints and a small brush. Some ideas include the following: beach with a lifeguard stand, blankets, and beach umbrellas; a sailboat on the water at sunset; the ocean with rocks jutting out from the beach and sea gulls flying above. One shell might show the beginning of a scene and the other a continuation. For example, paint a surfer waiting for a wave inside one shell. Inside the other, show the surfer riding a big wave. Allow the paint to dry.

2. Press the clamshells into the clay base with the inside painted scenes facing outward. Position the standing shells about 2 inches (5 cm) apart from each other. Decorate by inserting a few little shells into the base, off to the front side of the clamshells.

3. Allow clay to dry thoroughly. Paint the base, if desired, being careful not to paint the shells. Let dry. Then add some stationery.

Seashell Notecards

Create a special set of Seashell Notecards for the holders. To make each notecard, cut and fold construction or other heavyweight paper into desired notecard size. Arrange and glue a few small seashells onto the top left-hand corner of each folded paper. Form designs with the shells or shape them into little pictures. Use fine-line markers to add a few details.

What You Need

large clamshell

newspaper (to work on)

white glue

3 marbles or large beads

small seashells, assorted types (whole and broken pieces)

tiny pebbles

potting soil

several grapefruit seeds, packaged seeds, or small rooted cuttings from a plant

Shell Planter

The seashore is a superb shell storehouse. Next time you're at the beach, look for some very large clamshells. Then collect an assortment of small shells that the waves have washed ashore.

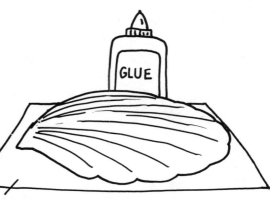

newspaper

What You Do

1. Place a large clamshell, hollow side down, on a sheet of newspaper. Use a large glob of glue to attach three marbles or beads to the shell. Space the marbles so that they form a triangle with one marble near the narrow end of the shell and the other two near the fanned out part. Let the glue dry.

2. When the marbles (or beads) are securely in place, turn the clamshell rightside up. The planter will stand on its marble legs.

3. To the outer rim of the large shell, add a decorative border of assorted colorful shells and broken shell pieces. Glue these shells to the planter. Let the glue dry completely.

4. Sprinkle tiny pebbles in the bottom of the shell. Fill the planter with potting soil. You're ready to plant your seeds. (Grapefruit seeds grow well.) Make several small holes in the soil, add a grapefruit seed to each hole, and cover them with additional soil. Or take a few seeds from a seed packet. Following the directions on the package, add the seeds to the soil. If you have rooted cuttings from a plant, you can plant these instead of the seeds.

5. Water your plant once a week, or when the soil gets dry. Give it plenty of sunshine. When the plant starts growing too big for the shell planter, transplant it to a flowerpot. Then plant some more seeds in your Shell Planter. And "root" for them!

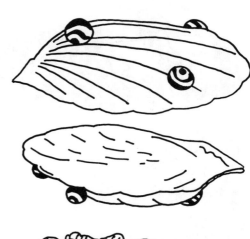

95

JUNE/JULY/AUGUST
ACTIVITY SHEET

Melon-Seed Necklace

Save seeds from watermelon, cantaloupes, and honeydews, and sew them into summer "fun" jewelry.

What You Do

1. Soak the melon seeds in water overnight so that they are soft enough to pierce with a needle. Then spread the seeds out on a sheet of newspaper to get rid of excess moisture.

2. Thread a needle with strong thread and knot the end so that the thread is doubled. Push the needle and thread through the seeds to string them. Here's a design you can try. String 1 bead, 15 seeds, then 1 bead, 15 seeds, and so on.

3. Continue stringing seeds and beads until you have about 5 inches (12 1/2 cm) of thread left. Cut the thread below the needle and knot the ends together. Tie both knotted ends to form the necklace. Make several more knots so that it will be securely tied. You should be able to slip the finished necklace over your head.

4. Create Melon-Seed Necklaces with some original designs. Wear one yourself and give another to your friend!

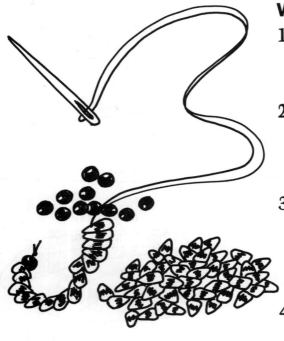